Qualitative Inquiry: Critical Ethics, Justice and Activism Series
Gaile S. Cannella, Editor

The **Qualitative Inquiry: Critical Ethics, Justice, and Activism** series is a collection designed to provide a cross-disciplinary overview of the use of qualitative research as an avenue for justice and critical transformative activism/action socially, environmentally, and related to more-than-human/human entanglements. Much of this work has been/is labeled critical qualitative research. Scholarship that addresses the complexities of ethico/onto/epistemological orientations in critical work is included, as well as both the diverse critical histories (e.g. feminisms, post-colonial/indigenous, poststructuralist) and contemporary becomings (e.g. counter neoliberal, decolonial, beyond human) that currently, and may in the future, unveil(s) power complexities and performances in ways that move toward more just transformations. Authors are invited to submit manuscripts focusing on the basics necessary for conducting critical transformative qualitative inquiry, contemporary views and conceptualizations of critique, critical research as direct activism, and critical scholarship that thinks research differently. Further, philosophies, traditionally unthought methodologies (e.g. counter and/or multispecies ethnography, diffraction), digital and media technologies as data and/or method in critical qualitative inquiry, methodologies usually labeled traditional that have been reconceptualized and employed for critical purposes, disruptive methodologies, and complexity methodologies like assemblage theories are encouraged.

Books in the Series:
Making Research Public in Troubled Times by M. Francyne Huckaby (2018)
Researching Resistance by M. Francyne Huckaby (forthcoming)
Employing Critical Qualitative Inquiry to Mount Nonviolent Resistance by Yvonna S. Lincoln and Gaile S. Cannella (forthcoming)
Exploring Data Production in Motion by Teija Rantala (forthcoming)

Gaile S. Canella (EdD, University of Georgia) is an independent scholar who has served as a tenured Full Professor at Texas A&M University – College Station and at Arizona State University – Tempe, as well as the Velma Schmidt Endowed Chair of Education at the University of North Texas. The editor of the Qualitative Inquiry: Critical Ethics, Justice, and Activism series is interested in reviewing manuscripts and proposals for possible publication in the series. Scholars who wish to be considered should email their proposals, along with two sample chapters and current CVs, to the editors. For instructions and advice on preparing a prospectus, please refer to the Myers Education Press website at http://myersedpress.com/sites/stylus/MEP/Docs/Prospectus%20Guidelines%20MEP.pdf. You can send your material to:

Gaile S. Cannella
gaile.cannella@gmail.com

Making Research Public in Troubled Times

Pedagogy, Activism, and Critical Obligations

Making Research Public in Troubled Times

Pedagogy, Activism, and Critical Obligations

EDITED BY
M. Francyne Huckaby

Gorham, Maine

Copyright © 2019 | Myers Education Press, LLC

Published by Myers Education Press, LLC
P.O. Box 424
Gorham, ME 04038

All rights reserved. No part of this book may be reprinted or reproduced in any form or by any electronic, mechanical, or other means, now known or hereafter invented, including photocopying, recording, and information storage and retrieval, without permission in writing from the publisher.

LIBRARY OF CONGRESS CATALOGING-IN-PUBLICATION DATA AVAILABLE FROM LIBRARY OF CONGRESS.

13-digit ISBN 978-1-9755-0028-3 (paperback)
13-digit ISBN 978-1-9755-0027-6 (hard cover)
13-digit ISBN 978-1-9755-0029-0 (library networkable e-edition)
13-digit ISBN 978-1-9755-0030-6 (consumer e-edition)

Printed in the United States of America.

All first editions printed on acid-free paper that meets the American National Standards Institute Z39-48 standard.

Books published by Myers Education Press may be purchased at special quantity discount rates for groups, workshops, training organizations, and classroom usage. Please call our customer service department at 1-800-232-0223 for details.

Cover design by Sophie Appel

Visit us on the web at www.myersedpress.com to browse our complete list of titles.

Contents

Series Editor Foreword   ix

Acknowledgments   xiii

List of Images   xv

Introduction: *M. Francyne Huckaby*   1

Section I
(How to) Educating(e) Critical Public Researchers: Pedagogies Across Disciplines

1. Thinking, Willing, and Judging in (Post)Qualitative Research: A Series of Resettings   15
   Mirka Koro-Ljungberg

2. Unruly Considerations for a Critical Qualitative Classroom: Teaching Well   31
   Jasmine B. Ulmer

3. Learning Is a Two-Way Street: Crossing Sociocultural Boundaries Through Critical Qualitative Research   45
   Joy Pierce and Luz Zareth Moreno

Section II
Sharing Local Critical Activism: What It Means for How we Conduct Scholarship

4. Research as Solutionless Participation — 57
   Franklin Vernon

5. Their Own Ways of Knowing: Art-Based Participatory Action Research with Refugee Women from Burma — 79
   Hillary Rubesin and Madison Hayes

6. Cyborg Scholarship: Films for the People — 99
   M. Francyne Huckaby

Section III
Strategic Next Steps and Obligations for Critical Qualitative Scholars

7. The Play of Seduction and Desire in the Making of a President — 123
   Bronwyn Davies

8. Nurturing Our Critical Relations: Research to Facilitate Justice Through Postanthropocentric Transformation — 137
   Gaile S. Cannella

AFTERWORD

Pedagogies of Hope for Dark Days: Talking Points — 157
Norman K. Denzin

List of Contributors — 161

Series Editor Foreword

Gaile S. Cannella, Series Editor

THE NEW MYERS EDUCATION PRESS SERIES, Qualitative Inquiry: Critical Ethics, Justice, and Activism, is a collection designed to provide a cross-disciplinary overview of the use of qualitative research as an avenue for justice and critical transformative activism/action socially, environmentally, and related to more-than-human/human entanglements. Much of this type of work has been/is labeled critical qualitative research, and is designed to directly address issues of power, oppression, privilege, and equity. We are excited to introduce the first volume of the series, *Making Research Public in Troubled Times: Pedagogy, Activism, and Critical Obligations*, an edited book by M. Francyne Huckaby. Specifically acknowledging the necessary roles of pedagogy, public activism, and critical commitments to justice projects that would employ qualitative research, the volume is an important contribution to the emerging literature.

First, the content illustrates movement toward increased justice in troubled times by making research public through deconstructed and rethought forms of pedagogy. Authors demonstrate ways to educate critical public researchers across disciplines by sharing examples of philosophies and classroom practices that foreground learning as interactional and, more importantly, learning as requiring processes of resetting, unlearning pedagogies like compliance, and rethinking deterministic pedagogical concepts like judgment and evaluation as unanswerable and unresolvable. Specifically, chapters address questions like: What concepts, practices, and challenges must be rethought, reconceptualized, even erased for the teaching of critical qualitative research methods that move toward equity and justice? How/what do I, or we, plan and organize? Can/how can these forms of organization facilitate/inhibit our critical research justice project? What have I, or we, learned over years of attempting to teach critical qualitative research methods and processes?

Second, conceptualizing, experimenting with, and learning practices of public activism are increasingly recognized as necessary for critical qualitative research that could ultimately be, or become, transformative. Here chapters involve sharing by activist local scholars who stay with the troubles even as they understand that critical qualitative work may always and already be emergent, contingent, and even solutionless. Example methods used to incorporate critical qualitative inquiry into community work, as well as what the researcher learned about public activist inquiry, are included. These examples range from researcher learning to "create film for the people" to issues of power and humility in research and support for refugee women (often identified by those in power as "the other").

Further, ethical critical qualitative research must address the contemporary problematic neoliberal condition, even global saturation, within which we are currently located. Critical commitments can include, but are certainly not limited to: addressing the neoliberal capitalist, postlife condition that perpetuates injustice broadly and in all environments, as demonstrated in the 2016 U.S. presidential election and the resultant attacks on people of color, women, and the environment; constructing uses and actions based on the existing body of critical work and methodologies that result in greater transformation; and discovering ways that diverse forms of postanthropocentric inquiry can be used to reconceptualize research purposes and practices that will facilitate more just ways of being. The authors in the final section tackle these ethical issues as they construct political qualitative research perspectives and actions grounded in hope for survival, justice, and equity. For example, neoliberal forms of seduction are countered as researchers are encouraged to acknowledge their own entanglements with contradictory forces that draw them into practices that create and alienate an "other." Scholars are further called on to always and already provide collegial support in a collective desire for a better future. Additionally, researchers' past critical relations and histories are viewed as facilitating new entangled becomingswith contemporary concepts embedded within posthuman (challenging human centeredness) and critical environmental perspectives. These unthought political combinations are put forward as generating possibilities for critical ethics and qualitative research as direct actions to counter current conditions in which inequities continue to multiply and justice has been/is being diminished.

As is demonstrated in this volume, qualitative research and scholarship that increase justice and equity address the complexities of ethico/onto/epistemological orientations. Diverse critical histories (e.g., feminisms, postcolonial/indigenous, poststructuralist) and contemporary becomings (e.g., counter neoliberal, decolonial practices, beyond human conceptualizations) are recognized as unveiling power complexities and performances in ways that move toward more just transformations. Authors in this volume were invited to submit manuscripts focusing on the basics necessary for conducting critical transformative qualitative inquiry like diverse histories, new becomings, critical research as direct activism, and critical scholarship that thinks about research differently. Refusing traditional and accepted linear approaches and concepts, the authors reinvent possibilities for critical pedagogies, activism, and critical commitments to justice. Using the volume as a handbook for rethinking and reconceptualizing qualitative research as a public project, the reader will be inspired and encouraged to take action. I am honored to have supported the volume editor and authors who share their work in this profound manuscript and that this particular book is the first in the series.

Finally, for the series broadly, we invite diverse critical philosophies, traditionally unthought methodologies (e.g., counter and/or multispecies ethnography, diffraction), and practices usually labeled traditional that have been reconceptualized and employed for critical purposes. Authors and volume editors are encouraged to take on disruptive methodologies and unthought transformative practices as their qualitative inquiry addresses justice, critical ethics, and activist research. The reader is invited to engage with this volume as critical entanglements emerge—pursue other volumes in the series—and to contact us with ideas for future texts and practices yielding just and ethical critical qualitative inquiry.

Acknowledgments

M. Francyne Huckaby

First, I thank Gaile Cannella for her support and mentorship over the years and through this project. I am inspired by her talents in bringing people together to think, build, organize, and transform, and I look forward to further work together through the Coalition for Critical Qualitative Research. I offer gratitude to doctoral candidate Ying Wang, for reviewing each chapter for consistency in formatting and carefully attending to citations and references. I am most appreciative of my family, especially my elders, in particular, Camille Pratt Truitt (mother), Mamie Thompson (grandmother), Sterling McCarty (Gramps), and Priscilla Tate (mother-in-law), whose beliefs in my intellectual abilities and pursuits have been so pervasive they took root in the core of my being. I am thankful and grateful for Brian Glenn, my spouse, who regularly nurtures me, making this academic life that I lead possible, and always supports my growth and flourishing. I would be remiss if I did not acknowledge my canine writing companions, Sage and Fennel, who regularly checked on my progress, as well as Coriander, who is no longer with us.

List of Images

Image 1.1.
Page 18

Image 1.2.
Page 24

Image 6.1.
Cine-eye-ear visual from presentation
Page 100

Image 6.2.
One sign from a series naming what
Chicago public school students deserve
Page 106

Image 6.3.
Project on Scalar
Page 111

Image 6.4.
Architecture of site on Scalar
Page 113

Image 6.5.
Presentation slide with words
Page 115

Image 6.6.
Notations for pairing screened presentation
with spoken words
Page 116

Introduction

> *The world has rarely been so much in need of people who can think hard about what's going on.*
>
> —B. DAVIES

Making Research Public in Troubled Times: Pedagogy, Activism, and Critical Obligations offers an antidote to these neoliberal times. At the very least, the book is an inoculation against impositions that seek to quiet critical scholarship and perspectives, dismiss education including the academy through transformative practices that most favor measured productivity and judgment, and push increasing numbers and populations of people(s) into the precariat (Johnson, 2014; Standing, 2011), a growing class of people bearing risks, insecurities, vulnerabilities, and dangers. *Making Research Public in Troubled Times* consists of three sections: Section I, (How to) Educating(e) Critical Public Researchers: Pedagogies Across Disciplines; Section II, Sharing Local Critical Activism: What It Means for How We Conduct Research; and Section III, Strategic Next Steps and Obligations for Critical Qualitative Scholars. Norman Denzin's presentation notes for his remarks on strategic next steps ends this edited volume as an afterword—"Pedagogies of Hope for Dark Days." Throughout this introduction, I share quotations from authors of the chapters to provide insights into their chapters and a sense of the book's essence.

> *We seek students and researchers who embrace a politics of emancipation.*
>
> —N. DENZIN

Section I
(How to) Educating(e) Critical Public Researchers: Pedagogies Across Disciplines

> *Rather than constructing and exercising judgment willingly according to institutional expectations it might be productive to approach judgment as a continuous "project"; an unanswerable task that lingers...*
>
> —M. KORO-LJUNGBERG

Koro-Ljungberg, author of the first chapter, sets the tone for the book—a series of chapters that reset critical qualitative inquiry—by introducing resetting. She writes, "When resetting one might have lost one's bearings but by taking time and following lines, processes, and potential 'instructions' to recalibrate signals, inputs, thoughts, and connections, affects and actions are re-created and reestablished." Chapters in this first section focus on diverse pedagogies and teaching practices that facilitate the education of critical public researchers, including judgment, the syllabus, and two-learning between research participants and researchers.

In *Thinking, Willing, and Judging in (Post)Qualitative Research: A Series of Resettings*, Mirka Koro-Ljungberg resets judgment through a series of 14 "resettings and illusionary connected fragments." Koro-Ljungberg's conceptual chapter brings thinking and willing in relationality with judging, and yet refuses a linear argument to define or operationalize judgment, or prewrite or rewrite existing and potential narratives. Instead each resetting offers another take, imagining "various theoretical, conceptual, practical, pedagogical, and performative elements." This chapter does not tell the (post)qualitative researcher, teacher-learner-practitioner, what to think or do with judgment. Instead it presents multiple takes to interrogate, with multiple angles and images, theorists and philosophers from Arendt and Barad to Wolcott, prose and poetry, past and current. I dare not say more about this chapter other than to encourage a reading that attends to what Koro-Ljungberg offers as well as what she makes possible for teacher-learner-practitioners as we open thinking, willing, and judging to resetting. Quoting Ricci (2016), Koro-Ljungberg notes that the "reset offers a possibility to render 'an instrument sensitive again to the signals it was meant to register.'"

In "Unruly Considerations for a Critical Qualitative Classroom: Teaching Well," Jasmine B. Ulmer begins with situating herself—in the world, a big world with comparable troubles, a world of human interconnected with nonhuman—as a teacher, who answers the questions about how she is best suited to make the world a better place: "by teaching well." While Ulmer explores herself as teacher holistically as elementary school teacher–instructional coach–leadership and policy–qualitative methodologist, this second chapter poses and addresses questions of teaching well for the critical qualitative research methodologist as teacher. Ulmer is attentive to the ways critical qualitative inquiry seeks to "destabilize hierarchical power relations," noting, "I am wary of teaching decolonizing approaches to inquiry only to risk recolonizing thought within my own classroom."

Taking up the syllabus as a concrete and discursive object, Ulmer reflects on the ways the syllabus reinforces and challenges institutional norms, mandates, preferences, authoritarian values, and disciplining rules even though it is a rather mundane contractual document. She takes the syllabus and the underlying classroom aspects that emerge through it as "opportunities to recalibrate our practices . . . as instructors of critical qualitative research." Her discussion initially focuses on "the rules that are," including how syllabi set up "Dos and Do Nots," pedagogies of compliance, as well as technologies of surveillance and control. Moving to "the rules that might be," Ulmer considers how the syllabus can foster unruliness, remembering her own learning with Koro-Ljungberg and her own "rules—or perhaps unrules" that she implicitly and explicitly explicates to unthink pedagogies of compliance with pedagogies of resistance and persistence. She points to the syllabus as an underutilized tool and potential site for ethical and critical action.

Joy Pierce and Luz Zareth Moreno in "Learning Is a Two-Way Street: Crossing Socio-Cultural Boundaries Through Critical Qualitative Research" describe themselves as humanist qualitative researchers and teachers of qualitative methods in communications (Moreno) and digital literacy (Pierce). Pierce, a professor, and Moreno, a doctoral student, both note their concern with social justice and marginalization, especially poverty in Mexico. This third chapter discusses the research process from entering and becoming engaged with a community to publishing. They claim, "We are committed to qualitative, more specifically ethnographic research. To do such work, complex and transdisciplinary visions are required."

Pierce and Moreno consider procedures for protecting human subjects in the United States, as well as Mexico, and the proliferation of qualitative research in Mexico in some detail. A significant portion of the chapter addresses impoverished communities and their roles in qualitative research and the need for qualitative researchers to respectfully and humbly become a part of the community. Pierce and Moreno write:

> There are challenges in doing qualitative research in low-income communities because it involves ethical aspects associated with the researcher's own prejudices, the care with which information is

documented, and anonymity, but above all else the ways in which dialogue and observation become research, because it is not just about using a method or technique but of documenting, describing, and narrating a human or group experience.

Here they recommend that researchers become apprentices of community discourses and practices before they begin a research project, stating that "making oneself vulnerable whether through attempting to learn to speak a different language—the native language in the community... breaks down barriers." The suggestions offered by Pierce and Moreno are respectful and practical as the authors recognize the need for continuous learning from research participants as well as students of qualitative research.

> *What may look mundane can, upon further examination, be radical, for sometimes it is the smallest, most ordinary interventions that become the most powerful.*
>
> —J. B. ULMER

SECTION II
Sharing Local Critical Activism:
What It Means for How We Conduct Research

> *We may resemble members of the communities in which we conduct research; however, the nuances of lived experiences may prove that race, nation, language, or gender identity is not enough to consider our researcher selves as automatically part of the community.*
>
> —J. PIERCE & L. Z. MORENO

The authors of the chapters in this section share their community, academic, and activist projects, explaining what the work means for critical qualitative inquiry. These chapters attend to the specifics of concrete cases to study sexual violence on a college campus, arts-based inquiry and participatory action research with women who are refugees from Burma, and filmmaking as activist cyborg weaving. The authors note ways in which their projects are situated with people in places where transformative work is desired. Their papers open up questions about solutions and the roles of the researcher as they share possibilities for staying with the trouble and coming to know the struggles (Haraway, 2016).

"Research as Solutionless Participation," authored by Franklin Vernon, argues for the necessity, value, and deep ethical considerations of solutionless qualitative research that refuses to fetishize problem-solving or solution-making. Vernon resists demands for conclusivity from colleagues who claim that "research(ers) shouldn't be involved in problems they aren't prepared to solve." Noting, as an illustration, the value of medical research into understanding a disease sans cure, Vernon explores and narrates in attentive ethnographic detail in chapter 4 the sexed and gendered injustices and violences at Galena State University (GSU). Drawing readers into considerations of "dissatisfying impasses or dilemmas" of underreporting and ignoring reports of sexual assault on campus, of refusals to add the simplest safety precautions, of dismissals of predatory acts, and on and on, Vernon writes:

> After spending the better part of the 2014/2015 academic year surveying students' experiences with and attitudes toward sexual harassment and violence, a staff member from the Dean's office published a damning report of student attitudes and institutional responses.... But she was told she could not form a task force on sexual harassment, and that the university would not systematically address the results of the study."

Through his presentation of the troubles at GSU, Vernon's work poses the problem that "Maybe this is how it has always been here, not a moment of crisis, but a way of life."

Vernon wonders about the usefulness of solutionless participation "if and how we can imagine solutionlessness and inconclusiveness as appropriate entrance and dwelling spaces for foregrounding complex perspective-taking and collective response through critical scholarship." He opens an entrance into "the aesthetic and atmospheric experience of the inescapable and suffocatingly specious neutrality of GSU culture that double-binds nonmajoritarian members of the community to unjust forms of endurance and academic death." Vernon invites a sitting within "circulations of injustices" to facilitate understanding of the dis-ease. Such knowledge is of value in and of itself, and no single researcher or team of ethnographers has the cure.

"Their Own Ways of Knowing: Art-Based Participatory Action Research with Refugee Women from Burma," chapter 5, by Hillary Rubesin and Madison Hayes, exposes problematic power dynamics in traditional research practices as well as their own PAR (participatory action research) and ABR (arts-based research). In this chapter, Rubesin and Hayes critically reflect on work that led to a partnership with the Newcomer Art Therapy Project and Refugee Community Partnership women's groups. Given that "post-migration stressors negatively impact mental health more than pre-migration or migration trauma," the projects provided the only clinical services and mental health support clinic in Orange County, North Carolina, specifically for refugee communities. Social work students supported the services and also conducted research. Given the impending student graduation, the women's groups were invited into PAR during the last four months of the project. The women responded affirmatively provided the research moved "*it* to the next level."

The bulk of the Rubesin and Hayes chapter unearths what the women meant by *it*, critiquing how researchers' actions obscured *it*, and revealing how an understanding of *it* evolved over the course of the project. ABR like PAR requires "action, responds to shifts in thinking, and assumes collaboration, connection, and self-reflection amongst both researchers and participants." Because ABR and PAR were central to the project, the misalignment and misunderstandings between project facilitators, researchers, and group members became clearer as the researchers and project leaders became more adept at listening to and following the intentions of the women. The authors write:

> It was the group facilitators who were out of alignment, operating under the confines of a strict schedule that provided little opportunity for the participants to exert agency over the research process or work within their own culturally appropriate timelines.

The interactions that aligned the facilitators with the women in the group and questioning the researchers' timeline resulted in a "dramatic shift in power and purpose" as well as a defining and refining of *it*. Interestingly, the women's original research question was ultimately reflected in the mission of the collaborative group that grew out of the ABR-PAR project. Rubesin and Hayes make clear the necessity of cultural humility and the problematics that a presumption of cultural competence makes. They note that the community of women knew their needs and what they were doing, stating, "Again, all the facilitators had to do was listen."

M. Francyne Huckaby bases "Cyborg Scholarship: Films for the People" (chapter 6) on her *pūblicāre* (Latin meaning: to make public) of the digitally born ethnographic film project *Public Education: Participatory Democracy After Neoliberalism*. She describes this work as "feminist research born of necessity" because continuing to turn away from it proved increasingly more problematic for her as a scholar and citizen. So Huckaby and her new electronic tablet joined the struggle for public education in Chicago during her 2012 sabbatical. Huckaby narrates the journey into researching the struggle for public education and becoming cyborg—woman and machine as cine-eye-ear—through the processes of joining and writing, rewriting as cyborg, and cyborg weaving. Huckaby as cyborg becomes the living participatory camera engaged in scholarship that is activism.

In creating films for the people, Huckaby explains how she translates theory into digital moving images, light, and sound to encourage "critical thinking through the senses" and make use of film's "capacity to disrupt past assumptions." Her films resist the typical tropes of documentary projects in that she gives full attention to "people in the struggle," writing, "I want viewer-readers to see people speaking about their experiences, explicating their own theorizing, and determining their solutions." This means she avoids authoritarian figures who explain and narrate, credentialed people who lend credibility, and famous folk who add notoriety, instead ensuring that her "films are diverse in race, gender, socioeconomic status, and roles." Such a move may create a feeling of absence for viewers expecting the talking expert who is often White, male, and financially comfortable. Huckaby makes films that challenge implicit biases about "who can speak, theorize, and problem-solve" and counter "myths of the hero, savior, or wise wo/man," arguing that such staples of films "interrupt and halt the communal work of knowledge-making and social justice." She likewise makes the absence of community sensed through moving image-light-sound that takes advantage of symbolic space and what she calls *symbolic illumination* to illuminate ways that connect individuals to collective action, noting, "This is a form of heuristic filmmaking. This is Black feminist scholarship. This is about survival. These are films for the people."

> *I wonder whether research can be valuable as dissatisfying and lacking conclusivity; as an encounter with precarity: an impasse that encourages methods of perspective-taking and imaging responses out to retrievable ends, where solution-making is decoupled but not distant from critique as a process of inviting diverse, collective, multigenerational effort beyond any one research project's capacity.*
>
> —F. VERNON

Section III
Strategic Next Steps and Obligations for Critical Qualitative Scholars

> *I, however, wanted to notice the people who were losing, refused to continue to lose, and chose to play a different game differently; those who exposed the structures and processes working against them and collectively sought out ways to circumvent, interrupt, redirect, and create anew.*
>
> —M. F. HUCKABY

The chapters in this section address the contemporary problematic condition within which critical qualitative inquiry is located and strive to facilitate action plans for scholars regarding these conditions. These conditions are the neoliberal capitalist, posthuman condition that perpetuates injustice broadly and in all environments; the need to construct transformative uses and actions for our existing body of critical work and methodologies; and the ways that diverse forms of post-anthropocentric inquiry can be used to reconceptualize research purposes and practices that will facilitate public transformations. These chapters describe major concerns for our contemporary times and focus on future steps, most importantly actions for how critical qualitative inquiry can be conceptualized to address concerns such as becomingswith politics of hope.

In "The Play of Seduction and Desire in the Making of a President," Bronwyn Davies moves between two shows—*The Apprentice* and "the very big reality TV show playing in the White House" to explore audience seductions by fictional heroes and the play of seduction in movement from TV star to president in a Trump-as-president assemblage. This fictional character epitomized the neoliberal survivor pitted against other individuals made more vulnerable, more obedient by neoliberal governments; Trump-as-subject-to-neoliberalism is individualistic, competitive, and without social values. On seduction, Davies notes that wariness of it does not eliminate susceptibility to it, how through it emotionality overrides rational arguments, how it enchants and denies things their truth, the ways it makes things into games, the centrality of narcissism in it, and that illusion forms through the death of reality. This seduction not only worked on the voting public, "Dupery was an art Trump had long practiced as a salesman, and the Trump-as-star illusion presented him with an irrefutable image that he too was seduced by," writes Davies in chapter 7.

Studying this "transformation of a fictional character into a president" has been made public, accessible, and transparent, quite possibly in a way unseen prior, given social media, what Davies calls "a rich seam of data to work with in analyzing the plays of power." Unlike reality TV shows that constructed a narrative and storylines (work that requires directing and editing), the very big reality show in the White House sans director airs raw footage of not merely surviving in this world shaped so pervasively by neoliberalism but succeeding in it. In this regard, the Trump-as-president assemblage seems refreshingly real to his supporters, whereas his critics await some sense-making of the chaotic stream of footage and data. Davies offers a close analysis of the *Access Hollywood* tape, to begin with a concrete case, as Deleuze suggests. This is an apropos choice given the continued rich data seam that stitches Trump-as-predator to the Trump-as-president assemblage. Davies's close analysis offers insights into how we might investigate our vulnerabilities to seduction, collective desires, illusions, dupery as she calls it, as neoliberal subjects, compared to the difficult engagements in work that is disruptive, courageous thinking "through the quagmire of power, illusions, desire, and seduction."

Gaile S. Cannella in "Nurturing Our Critical Relations: Research to Facilitate Justice Through Postanthropocentric Transformations" notes critical scholars' belief that such work could counter injustice have not born just transformation and argues counter to the claim that such work has run out of steam. Indeed those "who dare speak truth to power face increased objectification, silencing, hatred, and violence"—in these misogynist, racist, ultra-nationalist, crony capitalist, anti-democratic, uncaring, and increasingly fascist troubled times—as the existence of all living creatures and the earth hang in peril. Cannella points to potential reasons but focuses this eighth chapter on responding to the impact of "neoliberal all invasive capitalist patriarchy" and "reactions of human beings who have been unable to accept diversity, challenges to their own truths, or their own perceived loss of power," an impact critical scholars underestimated. Cannella attends to the possibilities in nurturing critical histories becoming(s)with critical presents and futures that yield not yet thought oddkin and transformative action.

She points to the ways critical inquiry, in consideration with the posthuman, can move beyond the privileging of the human. Such entangled relations with indigenous, postcolonial, and feminist of color knowledges, that have gone beyond the human, are locations of potential counter actions to the increasing injustices against "people as well as their more-than-human companions (whether so-called domesticated or wild) and the environments in which we all live." Recognizing critical qualitative inquiry's multiplicities and attentiveness to marginalizations as well as persistent, prolonged protest and activism, Cannella offers examples of critical qualitative inquiry becomingswith that have been transformative; it has not run out of steam. She instead argues that "we live in such complex and power-oriented conditions . . . that critical work has never been more important so must be continued and expanded" and points the reader in the directions of critiquing critical inquiry, acknowledging critical becomingswith histories, exemplifying critical histories of becomingswith, and nurturing further critical relations.

Returning to her earlier postcolonial/indigenous work with Kathryn Manuelito, Cannella reminds that in becomingswith requires opening up to the "inconceivable, impossible, even absurd" and remembering that challenges to human privilege are only new for the "dominant White, male West" illustrating "Navajo ontology as embedded within connection to the land of time immemorial"—a violently assaulted ontology. Cannella complicates these troubled times by noting the contradiction postanthropocentric neoliberal capitalism adds by centering capital and decentering human beings, nonhuman life, and the earth. As such, posthumanism can increase inclusion in becomingswith or "reinscribe exclusions." Peoples of color, in the latter, face further marginalizations and denials of centuries of knowledges— desperately essential knowledges. Cannella advocates for a nurturing of the former form of posthumanism as inclusion—becomingswith through "ontological transformations, ethical consciousness, egalitarian relations, and direct actions"—as answers to questions of "perspective, next steps, and actions." Such a becomingswith politics of hope in critical knowledge community(ies) is, as Cannella makes clear, always/already possible.

> *Without the expertise and wisdom of participant communities from the start, we often wind up diagnosing the wrong problem or asking the wrong questions.*
> —H. RUBESIN & M. HAYES

Making Research Public in Troubled Times: Pedagogy, Activism, and Obligations builds upon and continues the work of earlier critical qualitative inquiry as it sheds the naiveté the scholars in this volume, as well as qualitative researchers more broadly, had about the processes of change, roles of research, and possibilities of critical scholarship. The scholars here are posthumanist and humanist; attend to the human, nonhuman and more-than-human; make use of and challenge the West and Western thought; and bring indigenous postanthropocentric ontologies to bear to questions about research and the public. The notion of public takes on different meanings with each chapter, and while this book offers no simple answer(s) about what to do with research in these times, it proffers ways to reset and recalculate, provides inoculations and antidotes, illustrates ways to weave and seam, encourages forms of relationally and becomingswith, and demonstrates ways to resist closure and conclusion.

> *And the work has just begun.*
> —G. S. CANNELLA

References

Haraway, D. (2016). *Staying with the trouble: Making kin in the Chthulucene.* Durham, NC: Duke University Press.

Johnson, M. (2014). *Precariat: Labor, work and politics.* New York, NY: Routledge.

Ricci, D. (2016). Don't push that button!. In B. Latour & C. Leclercq (Eds.), *Reset modernity!* (pp. 24-41). Cambridge, MA: The MIT Press.

Standing, G. (2011). *The precariat: The new dangerous class.* London, UK: Bloomsbury Academic.

Section I

(How to) Educating(e) Critical Public Researchers:
Pedagogies Across Disciplines

CHAPTER ONE

Thinking, Willing, and Judging in (Post)Qualitative Research: A Series of Resettings

Mirka Koro-Ljungberg

THIS CONCEPTUAL CHAPTER brings thinking, willing, and judging into a relation and questions how one can potentially judge and evaluate contextually situated and shifting practices, processes, and outcomes of qualitative and especially postqualitative research. It imagines various theoretical, conceptual, practical, pedagogical, and performative elements of judgment without intentionally pre-writing and rewriting existing narratives and those to come. Rather than offering one holistic and linear argument, this writing introduces multiple resettings and illusively connected fragments constituting relationality among thinking, willing, and judging in various ways.

Resetting Judgment

Many scholars and activists desire and have the willingness to make research public even in troubled times, including present times of neoliberalism and other forms of extreme ideologies. To make research public often involves judgment of quality and impact—judgment carried out by scholars, academia, research funding bodies, and the public at large. Furthermore, the economic value of inquiry is being increasingly judged similar to the outcomes of research, validity of methods, forms of engagement, types of impact, and more. The ways in which judgment is practiced within different sociopolitical systems and diverse space-time also affect priorities and practices in classrooms, publication forums, and other spaces of scholarship and knowledge transfer. It is worrisome to witness how the judgment of (post)qualitative inquiry has become more and more standardized (e.g., through theoretical correctness, normative citation practices, and procedural assumptions). In addition, judgment and evaluation practices are also increasingly being shaped by specific institutional demands and conservative views. Rather than constructing and exercising judgment willingly according to institutional expectations, it might be productive to approach judgment as a continuous project: an unanswerable task that lingers and keeps educators, scholars, learners, and citizens sensitized to the complexities of researching, teaching, and learning. How should we (teacher-learner-practitioners) proceed and interact with judgment, what should be taken into account, and what could be ignored and potentially dismissed? What is being produced in this possible aporetic and undecidable state of judgment—when judgment meets its limits, potentialities, and (in)visible boundaries?

To work against different constraints and expectations set forward by neoliberalism and capitalism in higher education, I resist defining judgment (in singular ways) in relation to existing peer-reviewed literature and draw conclusions that could be applied across different fields where judgment can be operationalized. Instead, in this chapter, I reset judgment multiple times without proposing a conclusion, drawing from original judgment configurations, or extensively citing forms of past and current knowledge. Furthermore, I question how one can potentially judge and evaluate contextually situated and shifting practices and processes of (post)qualitative research. I imagine various theoretical, conceptual, practical, pedagogical, and performative aspects and elements of judgment without intentionally rewriting existing narratives and prewriting those yet to come. Rather than offering one holistic and linear argument, I introduce multiple overlapping thoughts, practices, images, and illusively connected fragments constituting a shifting relationality among thinking, willing, and judging.

Latour and Leclercq (2016) discuss the possibilities created by resetting. When resetting, one might have lost one's bearings, but by taking time and following lines, processes, and potential instructions to recalibrate signals, inputs, thoughts, and connections, the affects and actions are re-created and reestablished. "Nothing spectacular, no hype, no grand narrative, no bright future, no new agent of history, but rather a set of simple resetting protocols ... to see where it leads, what it allows, what it permits us to document" (Latour & Leclercq, 2016, p. 21). In addition, Ricci (2016) suggests finishing one's work, thoughts, and processes with a reflexive moment, which can define the moves for the next game. In this way, all is set for a fresh start without a new beginning. Resetting processes are also always nested within other processes. Before resetting, recalibration, remeasuring, revisioning, rethinking, revaluing, and more needs to happen. "A reset does not break anything; on the contrary, reset is a somewhat fresh term for something that does not refer to critique ... there is nothing direct, instantaneous, easy, in the apparent simple movement of pushing the reset button" (Ricci, 2016, p. 41). Reset offers the possibility to render "an instrument sensitive again to the signals it was meant to register" (Ricci, 2016, p. 305).

0001

Historically, judgment and evaluation have been taken for granted in many educational contexts, higher education, and classroom practices. Judgment is expected and sometimes even standardized. However, normalization and judgment of creative, postqualitative, arts-based, and often quite unintelligible inquiry and research-creation processes have been questioned and troubled in different ways (see Kuby et al., 2016; McNiff, 2013; Torrance, 2018; Watson, 2008). For Torrance (2018), evaluation, criteria, and judgment of qualitative research are connected to the political economy, governmental initiatives, and agendas. Seemingly disconnected and noncumulative qualitative studies can easily be deemed unnecessary because of their ineffective ways of studying the world, and, as such, they can negatively impact and distort the expected outcomes of economically driven science. Following Torrance (2018), writing this chapter and rethinking judgment in (post)qualitative inquiry might not be needed to begin with. Judging apparently disconnected scholarship and ineffective learning might not be the best use of evaluators' resources, and nonevidence-based forms of knowledge might not be worth the effort and investment (of diverse funding bodies). Yet thinking through judgment can be a meaningful and important task if only to engage in a dialogue with other scholars across disciplines and traditions. Cheek (2007) also challenges qualitative researchers to take charge of evaluation and judgment of their work before others will. The colonialization of judgment of (post)qualitative research can be a real threat and has the potential to shape the future (and the potential dismissal) of inquiry in powerful ways. A proactive and reflective stance might be one defense against the colonialization of qualitative inquiry, responsive teaching, and situated learning. Maybe it is time to hesitate again (see Cheek, 2007) and not be overly certain how to go about judging (post)qualitative inquiry and its various theoretical and performative extensions and practices.

0002

0003

Meritorious scholarship has been devoted and designed to set a singular or plural quality criterion for qualitative research (Cho & Trent, 2009; Morse, 2015; Tracy, 2010). In many ways, established and documented quality criteria would be an easy and convenient way to approach judgment: to compare processes and outcomes to the set and agreed-on ideal and desirable (e.g., processes, methods, practices, and outcomes). However, quality criteria are always situated in perspectivism, often representing the dominant power structures and widely distributed discourse practices and methodological hegemony. Criteria are based on shared understanding, agreement, and sometimes even forced group consensus. Additionally, criteria rarely take into account anomalies, differences, or the other. Therefore, approaching judgment from the perspective of quality criteria can be quite limiting and overly stabilizing.

It is possible that judgment produces a stop, halt, and possible ending to knowledge flow, sensing, doing, and living. Drawing from Arendt (1978), thinking also implies a stop. Pausing to judge assumes intentionality and careful attention to the task of judging. From an ecological perspective, thinking with and against judgment can create various instructional and pedagogical paradoxes because some forms of judgment might at least temporarily stop and confuse (i.e., by stabilizing unstable learning and unstabilizing stable learners). At the same time, one could argue that a complete stop (to judge) is never possible because even a perceived stop moves with the flow of the world, and the stop is constituted in relation to the events/things/objects/subjects passing by.

0004

Generally speaking, judgment is founded on an assumption that there exists an external (less frequently internal) authority who is morally capable of judging and that judgment produces something desirable (i.e., outcome, decision, position, points, grades, and sense of morality). However, in many ways, this type of judgment becomes challenged when the role of external evaluative authority is questioned or found insufficient and inaccurate. This questioning is especially pertinent when one approaches inquiry as an unintelligible process and always at least partially indescribable set of events and happenings. Traditional judgment calls for procedural transference and transparency and, as such, needs to be describable, linguistic, and communicable. For example, in many instances, instructors are still required to assign grades even though grading scales, rubrics, and other forms of institutionalized and formalized assessment criteria are always already failing and insufficient at multiple levels. Often judgment is not possible without achievement, a describable process, an expressible idea, or a rational proposition that can be shared and put forward for judging. This kind of judgment could be seen as limited and a one-directional exchange of knowledge because it might rely on conclusive reporting and transparent inquiry. Judgment might also function as an artificial blockage, forced communicative responsibility, and pedagogical intentionality, especially when judgment disrupts the flow of organic thinking, doing, living, and inquiring. What kinds of ideological and ontological assumptions enable judgment as a mediated standard and form of external evaluation exercised by experts?

0005

Many texts have been published about teachable conventional qualitative research. For example, learning qualitative research methods has been compared to learning a new culture, including new sets of beliefs, customs, and ways of doing (Morse, 2005), and the teaching of how-to research methodologies has been emphasized in many qualitative research texts (e.g., Early, 2014). Literature also exists on how to effectively teach research methods to students, including how to use poetry (Raingruber, 2009), how to use reflection as a tool (Early, 2014), and how to create meaningful pedagogical cultures (Wagner, Garner, & Kawulich, 2011). Some scholars argue that qualitative research is a craft and a skill-based inquiry (Hurworth, 2008; Wolcott, 1994). When research is viewed as a craft, it often calls for practice-oriented facilitation and judgment. From this perspective, skills are something to be passed on to others (future professionals) through normative social processes, methodological orientation and scaffolding, expert knowledge, and craftsmanship. However, too much of qualitative research is solely based on predetermined skill sets, clear techniques, technological learning objectives, or any other set of fixed, articulable, identifiable, and potentially measurable objectives. This kind of inquiry mainly produces sameness and normativity that enables judgment, and, as such, it provides materials and offers opportunities for external normative gaze.

0006

Hannah Arendt has written about different aspects of judgment and its relation to thinking and willing (see e.g., Arendt, 1978; Arendt & Kohn, 2003). Although I draw from her work, I am not specifically interested in morality or goodness/badness discourses and practices. Rather, I am drawn to the ways in which Arendt enables scholars to think about judgment beyond normative morality and how she promotes more complicated notions and practices associated with judging. More specifically, thinking, willing (i.e., the willingness to engage in the act, freedom of origin), and judging form the three pillars of Arendt's thought. Arendt (1978) draws from Kant, explaining that in judgment, the general (mental construction) and the particular (sense experience) are brought together without rules of application. In addition, judgment, as a critique of taste, works through an intimate and a private sense. Using this analogy in the context of qualitative inquiry points toward judgment, which embodies the mind and the senses (namely, taste), as well as the general and the particular. The general and knowledgeable of the inquiry and also the thinking-doing (Manning & Massumi, 2014) and affect (Massumi, 2015) should be lived and sensed when judging. In addition, this task or event of judging would need to happen without rules, rubrics, and predetermined steps or elements. For Arendt (1978), objects of thinking, willing, and judging are given in the world or they rise from the living in the world, but they are not necessitated or conditioned by either. Furthermore, Arendt (1978) argues, "the peculiar quiet, absence of any doing or disturbances, the withdrawal from involvement" (p. 92) serve as prerequisites for all judgment.

According to Deutscher (2007), who follows Arendt, to think requires readiness to think with others. Thinking also involves ambiguities associated with waiting: action by inaction. We must stop and think, argues Arendt (1978). "Judgment is confined neither to the role of spectator, nor to that of the involved party, but it must involve a thinking will" (Deutscher, 2007, p. xvi). Judgment without thinking is thoughtless. However, judgment is not knowledge. One can separate good from evil because one has heard multiple sides of the issue at hand and one can process that information. "Thinking results in no infallible or absolute truth, and judgment must surpass the thinking that engenders it, as thinking surpasses the sensory knowledge that engenders it" (p. 129). Arendt and Kohn (2003) referred to conscience as that which sits in "judgment in myself over myself" (p. 280).

So, if judging does not guarantee good judgment, and good judgment is no species of knowledge, then we cannot know that we have rejected or worked against ill. Judgment is carried forward by the "wind of thought" (Deutscher, 2007, p. 129). Deutscher (2007) further explains that it is impossible to haul judgment into conscious presence. Judgment is just made. For him, judgment is not a process but culmination. One cannot report one's judging because there is nothing to report until judging is over. Maybe this culmination is not even articulable. Judgment also often involves a leap. "The quality of judgment is only measured in terms of what you do in the event" (Deutscher, 2007, p. 135). Judgment is always a willing act.

Judgments reflect, build, and construct relational value systems and structures. For Arendt (cited in Kwak, 2015), judgment is one's ability to think, perceive, and understand things worthy of pursuing in a self-reflective manner. Thinking enables judgment, and through thinking individuals dwell on invisibles. Thinking is channeled into judgment through the mediation of understanding. Judging always concerns particulars and things at hand, and therefore judging calls for action. "The ability to judge does not aim at truth or knowledge, but the meaning or meaninglessness of what happens" (Kwak, 2015, p. 689). According to Arendt (cited in Kwak, 2015) judgment is not possible without imagination (to locate the generality of an example) and community sense (judgment being grounded in an anticipated dialogue with others, generating agreement with others, and begging consent of others). Judgment, aesthetic and political, is about taking care of the common world in which we live while ensuring the quality of that world.

0007

Judgment is sometimes situated within predictable moments and recognizable events, where the act of judging is executed in a planned manner. However, this type of judgment is likely to be incapable of functioning as an immanent critique or continuously shifting responsiveness because it operates through the anticipated presence of the norm. It is also possible that judgment cannot anticipate its needs or ways to know. Although judgment might imply an authority and a location of power, it also has the potential to serve as a productive reflective force, creating immediate change and opportunities for transformation.

Alternatively, judgment might happen in the name of ethical responsibility or pastoral power, signifying ultimate care and affection only to serve the betterment of the learner. 'I want to help you because I care about your learning. I also judge you since I am more knowledgeable and it is one of my tasks and responsibilities as your instructor, peer, or kin.' These kinds of positions and assumptions, of course, are based on hierarchical knowledge structures and the expertise-based accumulation of knowledge. However, if one sees knowledge as fragmented, shifting, and situational, then judgment grounded in accumulative notions of knowledge is no longer helpful. Simultaneously, the stable notion of judging subjects is also brought into question. An autonomous human subject (aka knowledgeable scholar or perceptible learner) is no longer capable of making independent, informed choices and wise judgment without being caught up with an error, interrelatedness, and ethical impossibility. MacLure (2013) writes about "wise judgements, based on the representational 'fetters' of identity, similarity, analogy and opposition, underpin the analytic enterprise as conceived in many methods textbooks and in our everyday habits as researchers" (p. 660); this is like that, this is a subcategory of that, and this is not what is really being said. In the absence of representationalism, the wise or pastoral judgment based on homogenous identity and knowledge politics is no longer possible or desirable. Judgment of this kind does not represent the learner's learning, meeting of the learning objectives, or teacher's desires. Instead, learning keeps failing, teaching keeps surprising, learners form infinite collectives, and teachers become virtual or imaginary. Maybe teaching and learning are re-created and revisioned in surprising and unexpected ways, which in turn would reflect proliferation of knowledges, lives, living, and ethics. Instead of autonomous and independent learning or teaching subjects, singular plural learner or becoming teacher could be actualized through foldings (multiplying and doubling of material selves, bodies, times, memories, and more) rather than splittings (a subjectivity divided into singular parts), similar to Braidotti's (2013) post-post subject. From this perspective, judgment becomes thinkable only as an always already entangled practice and folded subject, as Barad (2007) notes.

0008

(Post)qualitative research brings a whole new set of challenges to the practices of judgment, including differentiation, decentering of the human, infinite becoming of inquiry, subject, text, and diverse appearances of the difference-in-itself and more. How to exercise judgment in this context? For example, if judgment is a relational process, then it is possible that one might teach, learn, and judge with the ghosts (Derrida, 2006), through events (Deleuze, 1990), and one might collectively resist institutional structures by placing writing and curriculum "under erasure" (Derrida, 1997). Haunting and pervasive forces of previous scholarship, research, theorizing, history, and dialogue shape our presence and absence as learner-teachers. These complex forces complicate and challenge normative judgment.

Many (post)qualitative researchers' questions, negotiations, writings, and practices are shaped by the specters of other thoughts, linkages to other writers, texts, theories, and connections with anticipated and virtual readers. Past judgments also haunt us. It might be productive to imagine how complexities and simplifications of the past judgment might create new possibilities and impossibilities for practices of today.

0009

Deutscher (2007) proposed that judgment is more than the role of spectator and involved party because it involves a thinking will. "In judgment I express my pleasure in what I sense, but go beyond the fact of my taste, posing it as answerable to critique. I enter the circuit of reason and reasoning" (Deutscher, 2007, p. 138). To judge calls for the will to take a stance, think, and reflect. Willingness functions through its leap to the unknown. The instructor is willing to offer commentary and reflection spontaneously while working through materials and processes without any rules and predetermined guidelines, exemplifying various approaches to meet the unknown and other within oneself and elsewhere. Arendt and Kohn (2003) propose that "the will reaches not only into the future, but it is also the faculty by which we can affirm and deny... there is indeed an element of willing in all judgments. I can say yes or no to what is" (p. 283).

0010

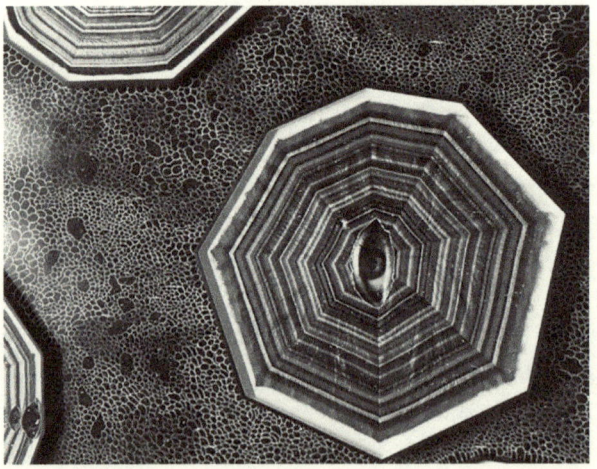

0011

For many of us, (post)qualitative research is nuanced, multifaceted, situational, unpredictable, intuitive, and creative, and thus it does not easily align itself with normative, predictable, or even humanistic/caring judgment. Willingly alongside postqualitative research, notions of fragmentation, uncertainty, movement, and various forms of entanglement transform the inquiry as well as the thinking, teaching, and learning of postmethods. Within these processes, willing subjects take various forms. Virtual learners and simulacra teachers stumble, stutter, reverse, return, and enter. We have more than one (method, student, teacher, content, goal, and judgment), and the state of singular pluralness (Nancy, 2000) unites learners, teachers, materials, and more than humans. As a result of this endless often material and relational potentiality, one begins to wonder what to do with judgment and how judgment might produce its own critique. What would singular plural judgment shaping learning-teaching look like? How might a multiplicity of judgment change classroom practices? How might research creations (Manning, 2016) be judged or what might judgment have to do with research creations to begin with? Should we simply remove or forget judgment altogether? It is, after all, possible that when we stop ruining other people's knowledges and their learning (see e.g., Lather, 2016), the only thing we have left is learning, teaching, and judgment halfway or in virtual form; not quite here, there, or that but somewhere and somehow still working and producing.

0012

Maybe judgment needs to build more from its continuous potential for change and even deconstruction. For example, from the Deleuzian (1997) perspective, judgment prevents the emergencies of any new modes of existence. Judgment is linked to the terror of expertise and the unquestionable dangerous powers of expert knowledge. Judgment cuts up the existing into lots, spaces, and units, which can be evaluated and condemned. Judging requires organization of bodies, and the only way to escape is to make yourself a body without organs and refuse to relate to others through existing social and educational categories. According to Tynan (2011), judgment does not mean the same thing as evaluation because the latter is proposed as the existential and creative element by which judgments are made possible. Whenever Deleuze (1997) denounces judgment, what is denounced is less the judgment itself as an activity of knowledge than the point of view on life, the mode of existence, that is presupposed by it. Every judgment of knowledge, in other words, presupposes a judgment of existence, a prior morality (Deleuze, 1997). Ultimately, what judgment means for Deleuze is not some system of categorical knowledge but a prior attitude or presupposition. For Tynan (2011), "The real danger is not judgement *per se*, much less evaluation, but this manner in which a subject find itself verified by its own experience despite the fact that subjectivity is nothing other than the synthetic construction of itself" (p. 58 [italics in original]). Deleuze (1997) challenges us to create different and new ways to judge the learning-teaching subject without presuppositions and confirmation. However, the question remains how one might judge that which enables judgment. Is judgment always functioning in relation to the intellectualization of educational cruelty and as an example of pedagogical terror? Might cruelty and terror work in productive ways or is judgment from this perspective always condemned?

In addition, the subject as an independent entity is also being reconsidered, and as a result, individual agentic rational judgment becomes questionable. If teachers and students are relational material beings, then how might judgment and its multiplicities become relational? How might judgment account for intra-actions especially within non-normative pedagogical contexts or educational places of unexpected novelty and surprise? How might students' and teachers' witness and relatedness be judged and by whom? How does rethinking humanist ontology shift practices of judgment? How might judgment operate outside humanistic discourses and practices? This dilemma is especially interesting because decentering the human also implies decentering judgment. This liberation of judgment has the potential to enable other similar, parallel, yet differing forces that produce relatedness, entanglements, and (public) science. Judgment could even function as a multidirectional force or repetition constructing differences in pedagogical relations, materials, molecules, gravitational forces, plant thinking, and space-time. Relational ethics would replace individualistic "goodness and performance" scripts, and the morality of educational subjects might be reconceptualized as part of the more-than-human universe. Rubrics, normative expectations, and shared and standardized learning materials become multiple and shifting—teaching and learning as we have come to know them through humanism and psychology collapse, and the potential void of judgment challenges our existing practices. Judgment could find fertile possibilities and ripe emerging connections within open and liberated universities, shadow universities, and public universities, which themselves live difference and multiplicity and embody becoming nonstructures. Higgins, Madden, Bérard, Lenz Kothe, and Nordstrom (2017) offer patchwork(ing) as a strategy and pedagogical practice for postqualitative research. Instead of methodological precision, the task of a plural methodologist or multiple de/signer has to do with a series of Derridian "scandalous sutures." Patchwork(ing) might involve theories but also other fabrics of life at large. Maybe judgment is yet another fabric to stitch together with anything and everything thinkable but more importantly unthinkable.

0013

Judgment is not bad or good, but it does what it does (see also Manning, 2016). To leave readers with some unsettling thoughts without a conclusion and to stimulate qualitative scholars to think differently about judgment and its "doings," especially in the context of teaching-learning-doing-living, I utilize what-if imaginaries. Drawing from Manning and Massumi's (2014) notion of possibility and their practice of experimenting with breach and potentiality, I offer some imaginary connections between judgment and life. Speculating on what-if thinking might be only sensed. Borrowing from Forsythe (2003), Manning and Massumi (2014) describe Forsyth's collaboration with a composer as not thinking but organizing bodies. From Manning and Massumi's (2014) perspective, thinking does not build from planning and advanced design but it happens in the movement and in the moving. What-if activates the past and history while "seeing what is in front of you." Speculative thinking carries unexpected forces and energy. "As-if: a mode that moves language to its narrative limit, pushing language to say not how if and then follow, but how 'if' becomes its own limit, a transversal limit that cuts across the if-then" (Manning & Massumi, 2014, p. 49). According to Löytönen (2017), what-if is a "question allied to the potential; the what-if question is tentative, open, and partial, drawing attention to connections, movement (flux), and the constant becoming of things" (p. 236). Löytönen (2017) refers to a series of "palpations (thinking-writing events) produced through in-between-ness, variation, expansion, and offshoots, with no line to follow to the end but accidental encounters, where something connects and forces one to think" (p. 237).

0014

What if judgment functions as autotelic activity...
>Flow and energy for its own sake
>Motivated by sense, movement, and transformation
>Without transparent intention and planned futurity

What if judgment functions as sense of accomplishment questioning itself...
>Overcoming oneself and moving beyond
>Celebration of work done, not done, and lives lived
>Old accomplishments generating room for other and becoming
>Response Abilities

What if judgment functions as tasting color...
>More and more unexpected
>Wild connections and productive intersections
>Sensing and knowing, living and writing, flowers and ants united

What if judgment functions as always more than one...
>Never alone but always together
>Never isolated but always united
>Never singular but always plural
>Ei koskaan yksin onnettomana vaan aina yhdessä toisiaan tukien
>Hyberobject—everywhere at once and infiltrating everything

What if judgment functions as ongoing entanglement...
>Texts, teachers, students, paper, ink, omission, wet tongue of the favorite pet
>Today, tomorrow, history, spiky hair, blushing face, running nose
>Home, work, school, house, bed, mattress, shining start, half moon

>And always more.

What might become possible?

References

Arendt, H. (1978). *The life of the mind.* New York, NY: Harcourt Brace Jovanovich.
Arendt, H., & Kohn, J. (2003). *Responsibility and judgment.* New York, NY: Schocken Books.
Barad, K. (2007). *Meeting the universe halfway.* Durham, NC: Duke University Press.
Braidotti, R. (2013). *The posthuman.* Cambridge, MA: Polity Press.
Cheek, J. (2007). Qualitative inquiry, ethics, and politics of evidence working within these spaces rather than being worked over by them. *Qualitative Inquiry, 13*(8), 1051-1059.
Cho, J., & Trent, A. (2009). Validity criteria for performance-related qualitative work: Toward a reflexive, evaluative, and coconstructive framework for performance in/as qualitative inquiry. *Qualitative Inquiry, 15*(6), 1-29.
Deleuze, G. (1990). *The logic of sense* (M. Lester, Trans.). New York, NY: Columbia University Press.
Deleuze, G. (1997). *Essays critical and clinical* (D. W. Smith & M. A. Greco, Trans.). Minneapolis, MN: University of Minnesota Press.
Derrida, J. (1997). *Of grammatology* (G. Spivak, Trans.). Baltimore, MD: The Johns Hopkins University Press.
Derrida, J. (2006). *Specters of Marx* (P. Kamuf, Trans.). New York, NY: Routledge.
Deutscher, M. (2007). *Judgment after Arendt.* Hampshire, UK: Ashgate.
Early, M. (2014). A synthesis of the literature on research methods education. *Teaching in Higher Education, 19*(3), 242-253.
Forsythe, W. (2003). "Interview with John Tusa". *Balletco Magazine,* February 3. http://www.ballet.co.uk/magazines/yr_03/feb03/interview_bbc_forsythe.htm.
Higgins, M., Madden, B., Bérard, M.-F., Lenz Kothe, E., & Nordstrom, S. (2017). De/signing research in education: Patchwork(ing) methodologies with theory. *Educational Studies, 43*(1), 16-39.
Hurworth, R. (2008). *Teaching qualitative research: Cases and issues.* Rotterdam, The Netherlands: SensePublishers.
Kuby, C., Aguayo, R., Holloway, N., Mulligan, J., Shear, S., & Ward, A. (2016). Teaching, troubling, transgressing: Thinking with theory in a post-qualitative inquiry course. *Qualitative Inquiry, 22*(2), 140-148.
Kwak, D.-J. (2015). The implications of Arendt's concept of judgment for humanistic teaching in a postmetaphysical age. *Educational Theory, 65*(6), 681-697.
Lather, P. (2016). Top ten list. *Cultural Studies<=>Critical Methodologies, 16*(2), 125-131.
Latour, B., & Leclercq, C. (Eds.). (2016). *Reset modernity!* Cambridge, MA: The MIT Press.
Löytönen, T. (2017). Educational development within higher arts education: An experimental move beyond fixed pedagogies. *International Journal for Academic Development,* pp. 1-14.

MacLure, M. (2013). Researching without representation? Language and materiality in post-qualitative research. *International Journal of Qualitative Studies in Education, 26*(6), 658-667.
Manning, E. (2016). *The minor gesture.* Durham, NC: Duke University Press.
Manning, E., & Massumi, B. (2014). *Thought in the act: Passages in the ecology of experience.* Minneapolis, MN: University of Minnesota Press.
Massumi, B. (2015). *Politics of affect.* Cambridge, UK: Polity.
McNiff, S. (Ed.). (2013). *Art as research: Opportunities and challenges.* Bristol, UK: Intellect Ltd.
Morse, J. (2005). Qualitative research is not a modification of quantitative research. *Qualitative Health Research, 15*(8), 1003-1005.
Morse, J. M. (2015). Critical analysis of strategies for determining rigor in qualitative inquiry. *Qualitative Health Research, 25*(9), 1212-1222.
Nancy, J.-L. (2000). *Being singular plural.* Stanford, CA: Stanford University Press.
Raingruber, B. (2009). Assigning poetry reading as a way of introducing students to qualitative data analysis. *Journal of Advanced Nursing, 65*(8), 1753-1761.
Ricci, D. (2016). Don't push that button! In B. Latour & C. Leclercq (Eds.), *Reset modernity!* (pp. 24-41). Cambridge, MA: The MIT Press.
Torrance, H. (2018). Evidence, criteria, policy, and politics. In N. Denzin & Y. Lincoln (Eds.), *The Sage handbook of qualitative research* (5th ed., pp. 766-795). Los Angeles, CA: Sage.
Tracy, S. J. (2010). Qualitative quality: Eight "Big-Tent" criteria for excellent qualitative research. *Qualitative Inquiry, 16*(10), 837-851.
Tynan, A. (2011). Deleuze, critique and the problem of judgement. *Deleuze, critica și problema judecății, 1*(2), 51-64.
Wagner, C., Garner, M., & Kawulich, B. (2011). The state of the art of teaching research methods in the social sciences: Towards a pedagogical culture. *Studies in Higher Education, 36*(1), 75-88.
Watson, C. (2008). *Reflexive research and the (re)turn to the Baroque.* Rotterdam, The Netherlands: SensePublishers.
Wolcott, H. F. (1994). *Transforming qualitative data: Description, analysis, and interpretation.* Thousand Oaks, CA: Sage Publications.

CHAPTER TWO

Unruly Considerations for a Critical Qualitative Classroom: Teaching Well

Jasmine B. Ulmer

THE TROUBLES OF the world often seem big—sometimes in ways that can be enormously and overwhelmingly so. It does not help that, in comparison, I can seem so very small. On most days, I am at a loss as to what to do. At the same time, I find myself contemplating two particular questions: (a) How can I help make the world a better place? (b) How am I best positioned to respond to the ugliness that can surround? Though I do not have good answers, I continue to circle back to the importance of classroom teaching and why it was that I chose to become an educator 15 years ago. My former self would have explained that she went into public education for reasons involving equity, inclusion, and environmental justice. In different words, she would have talked about how the various human and nonhuman parts of the world are interconnected, and how it is essential to act with care toward them all. She also would have shared that the abilities to think critically and independently are profoundly important skills in life because they lead to power, knowledge, access, and opportunity. This former self began as a reading teacher before taking detours through 2nd grade, special education, and elementary art classrooms; through instructional coaching positions in math and science; through state and federal policy roles; and through graduate work in leadership and policy—before heading 17 hours north on the same interstate she had been living near to become a qualitative methodologist. Teaching is what my past self has done in the world, and it is what I continue to do now. The response I came up with for both questions then could perhaps be expected. I am best positioned to respond to the world and can potentially make it a better place by *teaching well*.

It might be helpful to make explicit that in my own practice, I do not tend to approach teaching well as an attainable goal or destination. For me, strong teaching is a moving target—one that I hope moves back a little each time I teach. In this way, I believe that a growth mindset is important not only for students, but for instructors as well. This includes me. Further, in the opportunities I have had to learn from and with other educators, I have found that the best teachers often are those who are most willing to open up about their teaching practice through uncertainty, unknowing, and humility, for these are gestures that have the potential to create safe spaces in which we might collectively think and learn together. It is from these teachers whom I draw inspiration here—the educators who choose to make visible where they are in their thinking, the challenges they face, and how, in the process, we might all still have room to grow.

This can be particularly important when it comes to teaching critical qualitative inquiry. Given that part of what critical qualitative inquiry seeks to do is question hierarchical power relations, it can be helpful to consider how critical qualitative classrooms can contribute toward these aims. For without being thoughtful about pedagogies, critical or otherwise, it can be easy to revert to normative models of education in which educators (as the sole knowers) teach to students in the classroom audience, as if they are sitting passively waiting to receive knowledge. If critical qualitative inquiry instead offers a move to empower, engage, and think alongside students, then classrooms can provide significant opportunities to do this as well. As such, this chapter is a thinking about how critical classrooms might be constructed as much as it is a chance for reflection. Because authoritarian values often manifest within postsecondary classrooms (hooks, 2010), this is necessary and ongoing work. Apparatuses of power can emerge even within committed critical qualitative classrooms.

In part, this is because intuitional norms and expectations have the potential to set the structure, if not the underlying tone, for course experiences. In other words, what happens in classrooms is not fully within the purview of teachers and learners. This is not to abdicate responsibility in any shape or form, but to recognize that teaching and learning can, and often do, involve external constraints. Nevertheless, I would suggest that as critical qualitative inquirers, we are called as instructors to teach with the same ideals with which we choose to write. Identifying as a critical researcher does not offer inoculation against the ways in which our classrooms might have room to better align with the aims of critical qualitative inquiry.

Because I tend to think about issues of institutional power and knowledge alongside Foucault, here I turn to his concept of the apparatus. For Foucault (1980), the apparatus is made of "discourses, institutions, architectural forms, regulatory decisions, laws, administrative measures, scientific statements, philosophical, moral and philanthropic propositions—in short, the said as much as the unsaid" (p. 194). As such, I consider how some underlying aspects of classrooms—and how they can emerge through the construction of syllabi—can be opportunities to recalibrate our practice not only as critical qualitative inquirers, but as instructors of critical qualitative research. This, I would posit, is part of teaching well.

Teaching Well

I would note that my version of teaching well does not involve teaching students what to think. Rather, it involves teaching students how to think critically about the information they consume, including information that comes from me. This begins with a commitment to methodological diversity and inclusion. For better or worse, I likely have a "brand" of critical qualitative research (Cheek, 2017) that can be traced through my scholarship, and to varying degrees, there may even be times and places when I choose to build this brand. My classroom tends not to be one of them. To me, being inclusive does not mean only honoring perspectives that happen to perfectly and neatly overlap with my own sets of beliefs, personal, political, methodological, or otherwise.

As a qualitative inquiry methodologist, I have strong views on qualitative methodologies. There are aspects of methodology that I like, that I enjoy, that I am not particularly interested in, that I find fascinating and intriguing and want to know more about, that I think about every day, and what seems like everything in between. I attempt to be a respectful ambassador for them all. What I hope to be able to do as an instructor, then, is to differentiate between aspects of methodology that I like and aspects of methodology that are important for students to know. Those are two different things, and I am wary of teaching decolonizing approaches to inquiry only to risk recolonizing thought within my own classroom. This is especially important because, as likely is the case in many settings, I sometimes am the only qualitative methodologist from whom students learn. Not all students will have the chance to compare and contrast my own take on qualitative methodology with that of another qualitative methodologist who might do things differently. Though it would be easier to allow students to believe that qualitative methodology is what I say it is, and that the methodologies that I prefer are "right" or "best" and "most special," I do not believe that is what teaching well entails.

Teaching well, I would argue, instead involves being willing and able to teach across differences—including differences that are methodological. I have neither cornered the market on all that is equitable and just in research, nor have I reached a distinct plane of methodological enlightenment. Therefore, I would much rather foster multiple perspectives than allow students to believe there is one version of methodology (and that it just happens to be the one that I do). As a critical researcher who draws from standpoint epistemologies and situated knowledges (e.g., Harding, 1993; Rose, 1997), it seems wrong to suggest that there may be many truths in real life, but only one truth in my classroom when I teach.

Fostering multiple perspectives can begin with reconsiderations of pedagogical priorities. Specifically, these types of reexaminations can, and perhaps should, begin with a document that tends to be overlooked because it seems too boring—too mundane and bureaucratic: the syllabus. Syllabi, however, are more than functional documents. Rather, they are a form of discourse that emerges from competing priorities: They can reflect our own instructional preferences as much as they can institutional mandates. Through disciplining rules, syllabi convey what institutions and instructors believe to be important.

Crafting a Critical Syllabus

In writing this chapter, I often found myself returning to questions of how a syllabus can be made critical. In so doing, I realized that this was something I had not yet fully considered. So, I sat with it for a while, unsure as how to proceed. Then I tried something that, in retrospect, was precisely what I should have done first: *I located a syllabus*. It was not until I looked at one of my own syllabi that I recognized how many opportunities I had missed.

One of the things that became apparent was that I had focused on the big-ticket items involved in syllabus-making. I had conceptualized the syllabus as a reading list with related assignments that would allow me to meet institutional requirements and submit a grade at the end of the course. I had thought about the texts we might read, the theories we might experience, what we might do, how we might engage with (and situate this work in) the broader community, and how, in the process, we might continue to develop as critical thinkers, learners, inquirers, and practitioners. In other words, I thought about how we might productively fill a semester by doing what I was supposed to be doing, attempting to do it well, and supporting the broader objectives of the graduate curriculum in my program, college, and university.

Some of this work was indeed critical. Students were involved in crafting their syllabi before, during, and after the semester. Alongside students, I also carefully selected and examined readings through a lens that was committed to diversity, equity, and inclusion. Although these were productive and generative steps to take, upon further reflection, there were many other possible ways in which I could, as the session prompt suggested, "make a syllabus critical."

It is important to note that there is no one universal model for the syllabus that remains constant across learning contexts. There may, however, be commonalities. For example, I am required by my institution to include specific information on the syllabus, beginning with course registration and instructor information. Other mandatory details include course descriptions, outcomes, required texts, assignments, policies, schedules, and grading systems. In addition, required elements include boilerplate language from the university on policy matters regarding academic dishonesty/plagiarism, enrollment/withdrawal, religious observances, and disabilities. Further, I am encouraged to promote academic services available from the student writing center. Other institutions might require different things or require rigid formats that involve mandatory, fill-in-the-blank-style templates. Expectations for syllabi (and teaching and learning) vary.

As I explain, this exercise has led me to consider what tends not to be on a syllabus but what could, and perhaps should, be present. It has also made me think about how, as a former public school educator, my district gave me posters with predetermined sets of rules to attach to the walls. These rules were to be visible at all times, and part of my performance evaluation involved whether or not I had posted the correct rules, in the correct places, at the correct times.

Although I am no longer required to post rules on the wall as an instructor of higher education, I wonder if how we write syllabi is really that different. Whether or not we name them as such, there are still rules. Some are simply easier than others to discern.

Unruly Considerations

Classrooms at all levels have rules, whether we acknowledge them or not. This is something that I have continued to think about in the move from teaching elementary school to teaching courses in graduate education. I thought this would require seismic shifts in my teaching practice, and I was greatly surprised when it did not. This in no way reflects upon the delightful doctoral students with and from whom I have the privilege of learning. Not at all. Rather, it recognizes that the differences between pedagogies needed to teach 2nd grade and postsecondary education are, in some respects, not as different as they initially might seem. In particular, both involve a lot of rules, only some of which might actually be useful. To illustrate, I discuss the rules that *are* before getting into the rules that *might be*. Both, I would suggest, are constructed around implicit directions of what students should and should not do.

"Dos" and "Do Nots"

At the beginning of each school year, many elementary, secondary, and tertiary educators create a series of roadmaps for what (we hope) will happen in our classrooms. As much as we might like to think these begin with inspired visions for what students will learn, perhaps more often than not, the syllabi, lesson plans, and classroom posters we create may instead reinforce notions of what it means for students to successfully comply. Higher education instructors create syllabi to convey the institutional policies, classroom procedures, and elaborate to-do lists that determine how students should navigate a given course; elementary and secondary education teachers go to even greater lengths to convey expectations for how students should be, act, and even move. Much preparation and thought goes into communicating the norms of acceptable student behavior in P–20 education, some which I list here in a perhaps recognizable series of "dos" and "do nots." For example,

Do not be late to class.
Do not be unprepared for class.
Do not chew gum.
Do not eat or drink in class.
Do not leave the classroom without permission.
Do not reuse work from a previous course.
Do not submit late work.
Do not use cell phones, laptops, and other devices during class.
Do not distract others.
Do not use earbuds.
Do not wear hats.
Do not wear hoodies.
Do not run.
Do not shout.
Do not talk back.

Be polite.
Be respectful.
Dress appropriately.
Face forward.
Fill in the bubble completely.
Follow directions.
Keep hands, feet, and other objects to yourself.
Keep your eyes on your own paper.
Raise your hand for permission to speak.
Use your inside voice.
Sit in your assigned seat and remain seated.
Walk in a straight line.

There are others, too. These and similar rules are likely to be familiar to those who have spent time in the U.S. educational system (and similar systems elsewhere). This is not, however, to suggest that there are not thoughtful reasons for rules to exist. There are. Sometimes rules are in place for legitimate purposes, such as keeping students safe or creating welcoming and inclusive learning environments. Yet not all rules are created equally. There are other rules that are designed primarily to impress, convenience, or protect other parties by positioning syllabi as contractual documents. Because rules can serve a variety of functions simultaneously, they have the power to restrict, control, defend, facilitate, catalyze (and also all of these things at once). Some rules are concealed and others are overt. All should be thoughtful.

This is probably a good time, therefore, to confess that many of my own current and former students likely would associate some of previous statements with my teaching practices. For example, my 2nd grade students used to walk in excellent lines. Because other members of the school community judged the overall quality of the classroom teacher by the overall quality of the lines in which the children walked, this was a task that *we*—by which I really mean *I*—took quite seriously. Once we stepped outside the classroom door, I used my best, sweetest, most patient, outward teacher persona to underscore the significance of how we walked in line. And I did this to regulate and maintain order. Misbehaving in line was among the greatest possible sins of a child in that particular elementary school. I have since come to realize that, in many respects, the expectations of elementary students may not be that different from what we sometimes expect from graduate students. As the lone qualitative methodologist in my college, some colleagues hope and expect that I will be the one who keeps doctoral students in line. Toward this end, I even have crafted a mini-speech for students about "staying in your lane," which roughly translates into,

> I know qualitative methodologies are awesome and exciting, but please do not do ethnography and grounded theory and phenomenology and narrative inquiry and case study research in the same study. Choose one of these, or another methodology you like, and do that. You can even craft your own methodological design if you prefer. But pick a lane—whatever lane that is—and stay in it. Please do not do everything at once.

Although the fine print in this speech allows for off-roading and encourages the creation of new lanes, I am afraid that the underlying message may be all too clear, and that is: "Stay in line."

As students continue to progress through their schooling, one year carries over into the next as educational norms creep upward. I have to unteach, if you will, my graduate students: to stop regurgitating what other people think and start communicating their own thoughts. So, as I share that I will teach methodological approaches and suggest readings that may be of interest (or not), these are methodological choices and decisions that students will make. I adopt this stance because rules that are designed to create safe and supportive learning environments are too easily coopted into what I think of as Pedagogies of Compliance, and that is not my goal.

Pedagogies of Compliance

Pedagogies of Compliance are built from rules that are not always spoken out loud within P–20 education but can be present nonetheless. Here, critical pedagogy scholars might point to the ways in which classroom rules are mechanisms to regulate society (e.g., Giroux, 2011; McLaren & Kincheloe, 2007). As such, critical scholars within this school of thought might reinterpret the previous lists of "do" and "do not" rules to more broadly signal the following:

Do not ask (too many) questions.
Do not challenge authority.
Do not make noise.
Do not speak out of turn.
Do not stand up.
Do not step out of line.
Do not think for yourself.

Be where you are supposed to be,
when you are supposed to be there,
doing what you are supposed to be doing,
and only and exactly that.

Comply.
Obey.
Submit.

In these ways, macroeducation policies that aim to ensure that "no child is left behind" and "every student succeeds" can be bolstered by rules in which "every student obeys." Technologies of surveillance and control in classrooms are well documented, and Pedagogies of Compliance would turn the docile bodies of Foucault's (1991/1975) imagination into a permanent reality.

Whether we want them to or not, rules reveal our priorities. If my priorities involve critical thinking, then I would hope that the rules and procedures on my syllabus would work toward these aims. I found that sometimes, they did not. I now consider whether the rules I communicate function to open up or close down a pedagogical space, and whether I have thought through what each of those rules might produce.

Fostering Unruliness

Critical thinking perhaps begins in classroom spaces with a sense of unruliness. I was fortunate to have experienced qualitative research in such an environment. And while I hesitate to speak on behalf of other instructors and be the one to describe their pedagogical practices, I would respectfully share how grateful I am for having spent time in Mirka Koro-Ljungberg's classroom, where we were encouraged to,

> Read. Write.
> Experiment. Take risks.
> Try something new.
> Read more, write more, and then try something new again.
> See what happens.
> Question method/ologies.
> Imagine what research might become.

I continue to be grateful for each of these incredible gifts. Considering what I have learned from others also makes me think about what, in turn, I now pass on to my own students. It also makes me think about what sorts of rules, in the process, I intentionally and unintentionally create.

The next sets of unruly classroom considerations, therefore, are ones that I have been thinking about lately. These are the rules—or perhaps the unrules—that I now attempt to communicate in implicit and explicit ways:

Be kind.
Be thoughtful.
Be generative and affirmative.
Be yourself.
Be your best self.
Be situated within the world.

Know what is important to you.
Know what and how and why you think.
Think for yourself.
Think slowly.
Think well.
Consider the impact of your actions.
Resist.
Persist.

A dose of unruliness is important, I would suggest, because the Pedagogies of Compliance have led our world into a dangerous state of being. What we need instead—now—in this moment—are Pedagogies of Resistance and Persistence. They may lead to agreement, or not, or dissent, but this is what democratic dialogue is supposed to be. Although the democratic aims of critical pedagogy might aim to transform society on a large and sweeping scale, it is the more modest actions within classrooms that can make this happen. When we focus on teaching students how to follow rules—whether they be our own rules or the normative rules of society—we may be doing so at the expense of not only teaching critical thinking, but also fostering the sorts of critical actions that are essential to building and maintaining participatory democracies.

Critical Matters

Teaching and learning are complex endeavors, and are perhaps made even more so in critical qualitative classrooms. Critical inquiry is an ethical stance—one that calls for constant reexamination of how and why we teach. This includes syllabi, which I argue here have been underutilized. If every site is a potential site for critical action, then syllabi are no exception. Pausing to contemplate how a syllabus might be made critical has been (and continues to be) a useful exercise that has carried over into other aspects of my teaching. This includes not only what, how, and why I communicate with students, but also deeper considerations of how the work we do today potentially informs their futures as critical inquirers. The ability to think critically and independently—particularly when paired with a sense of unruliness—can extend outward in unexpected, yet significant, ways.

I am fortunate to currently work alongside so many students and colleagues who remain focused on how they might support others. Many explicitly identify this as their life's work. And it is through them that I more clearly see what critical classrooms can accomplish as students leave and ripple outward in the world. Like many of my critically minded students, I see inquiry as a way to advance democracy, equity, and justice. The difference is that I am able do so from a relative position of safety. When I write critical pieces of scholarship, I ask questions such as, How will this be read? In contrast, some students ask, What risks am I taking with my life?

It should be acknowledged, therefore, how much privilege can be involved in this work. There is a substantive range in freedoms which instructors are permitted across the globe. Although I am faced with constraints, I also am afforded openings upon which to build, particularly as a full-time, tenure-track faculty member in a democratic and open society in which intellectual expression and dissent largely are permitted. If I were to operate outside the boundaries of what my public university deems permissible, I might receive a warning or lose my position, but, as a U.S. citizen, I am unlikely to face interrogation, detention, or execution by my own government. Not all of our critical colleagues around the globe are, or have been, so fortunate. Teaching, doing, and even writing about critical qualitative inquiry can be an exercise in privilege.

We do this work, then, in degrees. Crafting a critical syllabus is not an all-or-nothing affair. And sometimes it is a reflection of where we are at and how much we can achieve in any given moment. It is worth remembering that the choice to take up qualitative methodologies can be a bold move in and of itself. Furthermore, statements of support or readings that are seen as diverse and inclusive in one context might quickly become dangerous or deadly in another. It is important to keep in mind, therefore, that criticality is not a competition, but a collaborative and ongoing effort; how and what one teaches can be highly mediated and fraught with tensions. As Kincheloe (2008) writes, "Advocates of critical pedagogy are aware that every minute of every hour that teachers teach, they are faced with complex decisions concerning justice, democracy, and competing ethical claims" (p. 1).

This work is not easy, particularly in a time when critical qualitative inquiry perhaps is needed as much as ever (Denzin, 2015). As such, I hope the considerations in this chapter may be a helpful frame for others across the critical spectrum in ways that may be big, small, and, for my students who take up democratic ideals elsewhere in the world, imperceptible. It is worth recognizing that critical classrooms can look differently in different places and still be significant. What may look mundane can, upon further examination, be radical, for sometimes it is the smallest, most ordinary interventions that become the most powerful. Teaching well—whether through texts, engagements, theories, or the tiniest of actions in unruly classrooms—matters.

References

Cheek, J. (2017). Qualitative inquiry and the research marketplace: Putting some +s (pluses) in our thinking, and why this matters. *Cultural Studies <=> Critical Methodologies, 17*(3), 221–226.

Denzin, N. K. (2015). What is critical qualitative inquiry? In G. Cannella, M. S. Pérez., & P. A. Pasque (Eds.), *Critical qualitative inquiry: Foundations and futures* (pp. 31–50). Walnut Creek, CA: Left Coast Press.

Foucault, M. (1980). *Power/knowledge: Selected interviews and other writings, 1972–1977* (C. Gordon, L. Marshall, J. Mepham, & K. Sopher, Trans). New York, NY: Pantheon.

Foucault, M. (1991). *Discipline and punish: The birth of the prison* (A. Sheridan, Trans.). New York, NY: Vintage. Original work published 1975.

Giroux, H. A. (Ed.). (2011). *On critical pedagogy*. New York, NY: Continuum.
Harding, S. (1993). Rethinking standpoint epistemology: What is "strong objectivity"? In L. Alcoff & E. Potter (Eds.), *Feminist epistemologies* (pp. 49–82). New York, NY: Routledge.
hooks, b. (2010). *Teaching critical thinking: Practical wisdom*. New York, NY: Routledge.
Kincheloe, J. L. (2008). *Critical pedagogy primer* (2nd ed.). New York, NY: Peter Lang.
McLaren, P., & Kincheloe, J. L. (Eds.). (2007). *Critical pedagogy: Where are we now?* New York, NY: Peter Lang.
Rose, G. (1997). Situating knowledges: Positionality, reflexivities, and other tactics. *Progress in Human Geography, 21*(3), 305–320.

Chapter 3

Learning Is a Two-Way Street
Crossing Sociocultural Boundaries Through Critical Qualitative Research

Joy Pierce and Luz Zareth Moreno

THE 2017 INTERNATIONAL Conference of Qualitative Inquiry called for interpretive, critical qualitative research that matters in the lives of marginalized people. We are humanists who conduct research and teach qualitative methods with social justice and helping those who experience marginalization in mind.

We each come to qualitative research through different lenses: a communication doctoral student with a theoretical emphasis in cultural studies through her studies and research in Mexico and an associate professor of digital literacy who interrogates digital literacy through social theory and critical cultural studies in the United States. We have similarities and differences between us, but we seek, through participant observation, to understand how and what we learn from underrepresented communities in an effort to improve their everyday lives in ways that matter to them. As we began discussing our approaches to qualitative research, we recognized significant differences based on culture and nation.

This chapter systematically discusses how we enter a community, become involved as civic engagement, and write for academic publication. We begin by comparing required preliminary steps for qualitative research in our respective countries. Background information contextualizes the processes we undergo before entering a research site. We then explain how we gain access to a community, being present and becoming an apprentice to the community. Last, we discuss publishing qualitative research.

Preliminary Steps

Conducting research involving humans first requires approval from an institutional body. U.S. institutions of higher learning call the committee that reviews these research studies the Institutional Review Board (IRB). The impetus for the IRB dates to the early 20th century. The National Research Council, a U.S. body under the umbrella of the National Academy of Sciences, Engineering, and Medicine, determines what constitutes true scientific research and what is considered meaningful research evidence. The idea for the council came during World War I and was made permanent by then U.S. president Woodrow Wilson in 1918. The intended purpose of the counsel was to "bring into cooperation government, educational, industrial and other research organizations with the object of encouraging the investigation of natural phenomena" (National Academy of Sciences, n.d.). The purpose of this investigation was to promote national security and the welfare of the American people.

In the 1960s, public outrage about the Tuskegee Syphilis Study, in which impoverished African-American men were used "to study the untreated course of a disease" and "deprived of demonstrably effective treatment" as to not interrupt the project (U.S. Department of Health & Human Services, n.d.), and Project Camelot, involving military and Central Intelligence Agency scientists experimenting with psychotropic drugs on their subjects, U.S. Army recruits, in part prompted the Belmont Report (U.S. Department of Health & Human Services, n.d.). The outcome of the 1979 report draws on practice and research through basic ethical principles—respect, benevolence and justice, and application—research tools, and protocol. Although IRBs were informally established in some institutions, particularly in the sciences and medicine, a 1991 mandate by 16 agencies that adopted the guiding principles from the Belmont Review as policy for the protection of human subjects, solidified the need for the IRB in all institutions of higher learning. This federal policy for the protection of human subjects is also referred to in the United States as the Common Rule.

Qualitative research is practiced in the fields of anthropology, sociology, communication, education, library sciences, and science, technology, engineering, and medicine. Because IRBs do not distinguish between quantitative and qualitative research involving human subjects, the same guidelines apply to everything from psychopharmacology trials (Lazzari, Shoka, & Kulkarni,

2017) to autoethnography (Chang, 2008). Protecting humans from harm is paramount; however, applying the same guidelines and measurements across paradigm shifts is problematic. Kamberelis and Dimitradis (2014) observed that "IRBs are made up of medical and behavioral scientists who, for the most part, conduct experimental research and know little about the assumptions, practices, and purposes of qualitative research" (p. 332), and the same observation can be made today. The ways in which some qualitative research tools are used and applied to what measures make certain required IRB questions and procedures extraneous (Bernauer, Lichtman, & Keible, 2014; Cannella & Lincoln, 2011). In essence, following guidelines historically intended for science and health quantitative research causes constraints in qualitative methods training, review of faculty research, threats to institutional autonomy, and inappropriate decision making by board members (Lincoln, 2005).

The General Health Law of Mexico, passed in 1987, establishes guidelines for human research in medicine (De La Madrid, 1987). The decree was reformed in 2014; however, the updated mandates do not apply to research unrelated to medicine. Qualitative studies in Mexico are recent. This area has been under development for approximately 20 years (R. T. Ramirez, personal communication, May 9, 2016). Disciplines such as anthropology, sociology, pedagogy, and recently communication, especially for marketing, have made more progress, each with its own history. In the case of social psychology, for example, it dates to the 1980s, and the terms of the debate between objectivist and interpretative paradigms are still being formulated (Cisneros, 2000).

A series of consequences related to the way in which qualitative research is carried out in Mexico derived from a brief journey that includes:

- No certification program like a Collaborative Institutional Training Initiative;
- Research projects that are unsupervised by committees of ethics in universities (at least not in communication);
- Informed consent not being a requirement;
- Acceptance of research projects made based on criteria of each university, with some more formal than others; and
- Project research requiring authorization by the leaders or authorities of social groups to be studied.

In the case of Anahuac University, the validation comes from forceful and rigorous investigation, in addition to the committees of publications of academic journals and books (R. T. Ramirez, personal communication, December 11, 2017).

During the 1970s, several qualitative studies had as a theoretical basis the sociology of development and the theory of dependence, as well as various interpretations of Marxism that contributed to the theoretical pluralism that was witnessed in the 1980s (Cisneros, 2000). In Orozco's (1997) words, the opening and inclusion of the qualitative "was not only due to an intrinsic development of the philosophy of knowledge, of the philosophy of science: it was due to the change of mindset among those who do the sciences, understood as hard sciences and the scientific communities" (p. 67).

Since then, Latin American researchers have been increasing their popularity and adherence to the qualitative perspective. Studies in the field of communication and culture have been notable (Orozco, 1997). The studies of Rossana Reguillo with regard to collective identities and youth cultures in 1991 or her works in the area of the social communication, within which she highlights that of recovery on the collective experience of the disaster caused by gas explosions in the city of Guadalajara in the year 1992, are carried out from a socioethnographic perspective (cited in Cisneros, 2000).

From the critical perspective, the culture of contemporary research in Mexico has formed a group comprising communicators, sociologists, and anthropologists whose last work (Galindo, 1998; cited in Cisneros, 2000) aims to present the main aspects of the research carried out from the following sources: surveys and qualitative interviews, discussion groups, discourse analysis, historical research, oral and life histories, ethnography, participatory action research, and a ethnomethodology approach to visual semantic analysis.

As for the ethnographic tradition in the field of anthropology, the investigation of the dynamics of poverty in Mexico realized by Lewis (1961) deserves special recognition. His work has transcended others because he focuses on the family as a unit of study, being a small social system in which "you see individuals as they live and work together, instead of seeing them as averages or stereotypes implicit in the reports on cultural patterns" (Lewis, 1961, p. 18).

Lewis's (1961) research is also important because of the incorporation of the Rashomon technique, which involves seeing the family through the eyes of each of its members, so Lewis is not limited solely to interviews and observation. Thus, it can be asserted that the qualitative approaches are extremely rich in possibilities to know and understand the social action of social subjects at a disadvantage and at risk (Arzate, 2007).

The development of qualitative research in communication is still incipient due, among other factors, to the long validation and trajectory of a positivist vision of social research that has caused researchers to believe that the quantitative perspective is more true than qualitative; the insecurity of the researchers in communication for the recent development of the qualitative; the hiring, financing, and encouragement to work using hard data; and finally seeing the qualitative as a speculation or as a fill, the latter in mixed-methods research (R. T. Ramirez, personal communication, December 11, 2017).

Gaining Access

When doing qualitative research in a low-income community, it is important to consider that poverty is a highly complex, socially constructed phenomenon. Inequalities are not only understood as a system of income-centric differences but as systems composed of situations of exclusion, discrimination, and exploitation (Arzate, 2007; Galindo, Sanders, & Abel, 2017). From the governmental point of view, poverty includes various components or dimensions because it is a multidimensional phenomenon that cannot be considered, solely and exclusively, by the goods and services that can be acquired in the market. These goods and services include the current income per capita, the average educational lag in the home, access to health services, access to social security, quality and spaces of housing, access to basic services in housing, access to food, and the degree of social cohesion (Consejo Nacional de Evaluación de la Política de Desarrollo Social, n.d.; Giddens & Sutton, 2017).

Despite eradication programs implemented by the U.S. and Mexican governments, poverty remains in both countries. Poverty reached more than 100 million people at the close of 2014, equivalent to 84.3% of the population, which is in accordance with Julio Boltvinik (cited in Reyna, 2015). Such numbers make it clear that we need to address inequality from qualitative perspectives through dialogue with the social (Arzate, 2007). This viewpoint offers a less cold and more humane view of how poverty is perceived and lived among those who suffer it. Quantitative studies are insufficient to reveal the situation's complexity because inequalities are in the daily living of life and go beyond the mere numbers associated with the world of work or the economic sphere. The study of someone's everyday life while living in poverty provides nuances that can only be captured at the microlevel.

We agree that gaining access to marginalized communities has its challenges despite our standpoint epistemologies. We may resemble members of the communities in which we conduct research; however, the nuances of lived experiences may prove that race, nation, language, or gender identity is not enough to consider our researcher selves as automatically part of the community (Filmer, Pierce, & Dolan, 2006; Pierce, 2006). To understand the culture of poor and undereducated participants, it is necessary to take time to learn their habits and the ways their lives are already changing based on their struggles and objectives. In the words of Lewis (1961), "to understand the culture of the poor it is necessary to live with them, learn their language and customs and identify with their problems and aspirations" (p. 17).

Conducting qualitative research in low-income communities is challenging because it involves ethical aspects associated with the researcher's own prejudices, the care with which information is documented, anonymity, and above all else, the ways in which dialogue and observation become research (Pierce, 2015): It is not just about using a method or technique but of documenting, describing, and narrating a human or group experience (R. T. Ramirez, personal communication, December 11, 2017). It is important to keep an open mind in the world of life, using reflection and reflexivity as a sensitive approach characterized by an ethical-political rethinking of the reality and the other as a human mirror of itself. Reflection, reflexivity, and empathy help to think critically of how social actors build around and live consciously with the risk, precariousness, violence, and socioeconomic inequality (Arzate, 2007) that is a part of their everyday lives.

Hence, before engaging in research, building a relationship with the community as an apprentice of their discourses and practices is recommended. Help where needed if possible, even if the work is not directly related to the research. One way to become an apprentice is by doing collaborative work. The term *human subjects*, the preferred term by the IRB, is replaced with *participants* or *coparticipants* as the researcher becomes more engaged with the community and makes him- or herself vulnerable to the research community. Making oneself vulnerable, whether through attempting to learn to speak a different language—the native language in the community—or asking questions about an unknown area that is familiar to a participant breaks down barriers. Gaining access in low-income communities is better done through an organization, institution, or person who is familiar with the group (someone they trust). Another approach is to shadow an established volunteer. The volunteers need not be a community leader but someone who is respected by the community. Finally, humbly approach participants.

Research Perceptions

Asking someone to expose his or her thoughts or habits, particularly when the interviewer and participant do not share the same socioeconomic status, can cause unintended tension. One way to lessen potential discomfort is by conducting the interview where the participant feels most comfortable. That may be in the home, a park, a community center, or even a bar. Wherever the place, it is likely that being in the environment will bring some source of comfort to the participant. While interviewing, talk less, smile more, and refrain from adding commentary about a participant's choices, struggles, or perceived wrongdoings. Some participants may be illiterate and thus intimidated by an educated researcher, and others may not want to acknowledge their lack of education. Poor and undereducated individuals are fully aware of prejudices and stereotypes, which may create hostility or defensiveness if the researcher is perceived as showing lifestyle disapproval. The beauty and challenges of qualitative research and microanalyses are that every interview—even if with the same individual on a different day—is unique and irreplaceable.

Qualitative research involving underrepresented U.S. populations, particularly ethnographic and autographic work, has gained popularity and respect in the United States in recent decades. Traditional quantitative researchers across disciplines recognize the value of qualitative methods and engage in mixed methods through collaborative research. Quantitative, rhetorical, and mixed methods are popular among new media scholars. The importance shifts from technology (tools) to a person's ability and technological needs in digital literacy scholarship. There are a broader range of methodological approaches, yet qualitative research is generally the primary method.

The perception of ethnographic research of this nature (underserved population) by colleagues/committee members in Mexico represents three points of view that attribute poverty to:

1. Individual causes and stigmatization of the poor;
2. Social dimension and structural reasons; and
3. A process that passes for different phases, marked by disruptions and lack of coordination.

The first point of view highlights the naturalization of inequality and high levels of inequality acceptance in Mexican society. The second locates poverty in the social structure and in its relation with other social groups. Finally, the third considers a historical and social process in which thinking about social justice and a better world becomes possible. However,

> societies such as those in Mexico, where social distances are not only widely tolerated by most social classes but lived daily as natural, and where social protections destined for the most disadvantaged sectors don't constitute rights but aid, scarce and of low quality. The risks of social fracture are increased and the opportunities of belonging to a society of equals become increasingly distant. (Bayón, 2012, p. 161)

Publishing and the Future

Thinking about qualitative research beyond paradigm shifts is necessary. Ethnographic research is finding its way in traditionally quantitative research and fields like science and health (e.g., journals such as *CBE Life Sciences* and *Qualitative Health Research*) and communication and fine arts (e.g., *Journal of Applied Communication Research* and *Critical Arts South-North Cultural and Media Studies*), indicating movement across boundaries. Furthermore, a greater number of highly regarded interdisciplinary and method-specific journals emerged in the last two decades (e.g., *Social Identities, Cultural Studies <=> Critical Methodologies, Qualitative Inquiry,* and *Research on Language and Social Interaction*), publishing important, provocative, and sometimes experimental qualitative research. We are committed to this trend of qualitative inquiry—more specifically, ethnographic research. To do such work requires complex and transdisciplinary visions that recognize there is always more to learn from students in the classroom as well as illiterate research participants. In Mexico, more qualitative research training is needed, so the method lives on (R. T. Ramirez, personal communication, December 11, 2017) because it is more than a technique: It is a way of life. The reflection of humanists and social scientists around values such as the dignity of people, equity, and social justice cannot and should not be sidelined in qualitative research; these transcendent values function as an epistemic framework of all methodological approaches. Studying human misery, understood as systems of social vulnerability, leads us to question the forms of postmodernity and their processes. Such work implies reflexively thinking of our position as investigators but especially as human beings. Any technical design that tries to understand social precariousness in any of its forms should carry these values (Arzate, 2007).

References

Arzate, J. (2007). Los métodos cualitativos de investigación y la construcción social del conocimiento sobre la desigualdad. *ORBIS/Ciencias Humanas, 2*(6). Retrieved from http://www.revistaorbis.org.ve/pdf/6/6Art1.pdf

Bayón, M. C. (2012). El lugar de los pobres: espacio, representaciones sociales y estigmas en la ciudad de *México. Revista mexicana de sociología, 71*(1), 133-166. Retrieved from http://www.scielo.org.mx/scielo.php?script=sci_arttext&pid=S0188-25032012000100005&lng=es&tlng=es

Bernauer, J., Lichtman, M., & Keible, V. (2014, January). *Qualitative research and the IRB: Where is the control group? A play in three acts.* Paper presented at the Qualitative Report Conference, Fort Lauderdale, FL.

Cannella, G., & Lincoln Y. (2011). Ethics, research regulations and critical social science. In N. L. Denzin (Ed.), *The Sage handbook of qualitative research* (pp. 81-91). Thousand Oaks, CA: Sage.

Chang, H. (2008). *Autoethnography as method.* Walnut Creek, CA: Left Coast Press.

Cisneros, C. (2000). La investigación social cualitativa en México. *Qualitative Social Research, 1.* Retrieved from http://www.qualitative-research.net/index.php/fqs/article/view/1112/2461

Consejo Nacional de Evaluación de la Política de Desarrollo Social. (n.d.). *Obtenido de Medición de la pobreza.* Retrieved from http://www.coneval.org.mx/Medicion/MP/Paginas/Que-es-la-medicion-multidimensional-de-la-pobreza.aspx

De La Madrid, M. (1987). *Regulations of the general law of health in matters of research for health.* Mexico City, Mexico: Official Gazette of the Federation. Retrieved from http://www.ordenjuridico.gob.mx/Documentos/Federal/html/w088535.html

Filmer, A., Pierce, J., & Dolan, K. (2006, November). *Confronting difference as qualitative researchers: Authoethnography as a site for intervention, connection, action.* Paper presented at the National Communication Association annual meeting, San Antonio, TX.

Galindo, C., Sanders, M., & Abel, Y. (2017). Transforming educational experiences in low-income communities: A qualitative case study of social capital in a full-service community school. *American Educational Research Journal, 54*(1), 140S-163S.

Giddens, A., & Sutton, P. W. (2017). *Essential concepts in sociology* (2nd ed.). Hoboken, NJ: Wiley.

Kamberelis, G., & Dimitradis, G. (2014). Focus group research: Retrospect and prospect. In P. Leavy (Ed.), *The Oxford handbook of qualitative research* (pp. 315-320). New York, NY: Oxford University Press.

Lazzari, C., Shoka, A., & Kulkarni, K. (2017). Are psychiatric hospitals and psychopharmacology the ultimate remedies for social problems? *International Journal of Medical Research and Pharmaceutical Sciences, 4*(3), 38-44.

Lewis, O. (1961). *Antropología de la pobreza.* México: Fondo de Cultura Económica (FCE).

Lincoln, Y. (2005). Institutional review boards and methodological conservatism: The challenge to and from phenomenological paradigms. In N. K. D. Y. S. Lincoln (Ed.), *The Sage handbook of qualitative research* (pp. 165-181). Thousand Oaks, CA: Sage.

National Academy of Sciences. (n.d.). *History: The organization of the National Research Council.* Retrieved from http://www.nasonline.org/about-nas/history/archives/milestones-in-NAS-history/organization-of-the-nrc.html?referrer=https://www.google.com/

Orozco, G. (1997). *La investigación en comunicación desde la perspectiva cualitativa.* Guadalajara, Mexico: Instituto Mexicano para el Desarrollo Comunitario.

Pierce, J. (2006). *Communication unplugged: A qualitative analysis of the digital divide.* Unpublished doctoral dissertation, University of Illinois, Urbana-Champaign.

Pierce, J. (2015). *Digital fusion: A society beyond blind inclusion.* New York, NY: Peter Lang.

Reyna, J. (2015). Cien millones de mexicanos en la pobreza, afirma Julio Boltvinik. *La Jornada.* Retrieved from http://www.jornada.unam.mx/2015/07/22/economia/027n3eco

U.S. Department of Health & Human Services. (n.d.). *The Belmont Report: Ethical principles and guidelines for the protection of human subjects of research.* Retrieved from https://www.hhs.gov/ohrp/regulations-and-policy/belmont-report/index.html

Section II

Sharing Local Critical Activism:
What It Means for How We Conduct Scholarship

CHAPTER 4

Research as Solutionless Participation

Franklin Vernon

I AM THINKING and writing within the logics, narratives, and projects of 2017 and 2018 in the United States. It sure seems like existence—at least the partial or limited constellation of life-making projects I have access to readily imagine—is fucked. Or maybe existence was already and always fucked. Or maybe I am alive amidst, among other troubles, a desperate and oddly explicit flailing of Whiteness and late liberalism; an overplayed demand for centrality mounted against a growing chorus for equity and decolonization (a project Whiteness may not be—is probably not—equipped to participate in without earnest cultural change), and it rapidly took on the semblance of a chaotic, irrational-even-by-human-standards tragicomedy. Cycles of colonization and abandonment, colonization and abandonment—that is the legacy and method of the culture I have been born into, and that appears to be maintaining its trajectory. Violent demands for centrality, suspended invisible to itself in the comfort of vacuous inherence (Yancy, 2004), until colonized spaces become untenable and are abandoned or made to die (see also Povinelli, 2011), because Whiteness would rather declare a space dead or meaningless than be made visible and a partial or shared claimant to meaning-making. Thus, as if maybe I exist in a historical present, at a demarcating something; an event, that feels like a period of crisis ordinariness (Berlant, 2011), which we will later grasp as an experience; a meaningful experience, and label as a transition with the violence of all transitions (see also Dewey, 1929), between this and after. I feel I am waiting for the declaration of death, of bankruptcy, of the always-backgrounded threat to declare the nihilistic historization that so often serves White declarations of the end of a cultural-historical project (cf. Gutierrez, 2017), potentiating horizonal projects of colonization to begin anew. But maybe I am only recently waking into the confusion, and fear, and anger, and sweltering ubiquity of the piling on of precarity (Kendall, Vernon, Goerisch, Kim, & Wolfgram, 2015) that already polices the spaces in which so many live and die at the discretion of majoritarianism (Povinelli, 2011). I expect at any moment to look around, adrift in the swirl and confusion of our current moment, and find I am only just now joining the party; unfashionably late to the ongoing reality of being alternately colonized and abandoned in perpetuity. Maybe this is how it has always been here, not as a moment of crisis, but as a way of life (Roitman, 2014).

The question of what role research—not as a thing of definite dimensions but as contested and contestable polysemic cultural-historical activities claimed and constituted across constellated communities (see also Rogoff & Angelillo, 2002)—may play or, more likely, be allowed to play or made to play in these times has preoccupied me. The genre of research I am focusing on in this chapter may be loosely referred to as "social science": the purposeful exploration and explication, however that is taken up in a community of research practice, of aspects of social existence thought made accessible and understandable by their methods of inquiry. I have been observing and living among two not-unrelated movements in the social sciences: a growing demand or expectation, often through being called to response by colleagues at conferences or through journal reviewers, to participate in solution-making as an obliged partner to critique as part of the price of admission into the research communities I populate (because research[ers] should be agents of progress or shouldn't be involved in problems they aren't prepared to help solve), and a fetishization of problem solving or solution-making absent deep ethical consideration, such as my students and colleagues in the public health fields increasingly identifying their research activities as "population management" or the building of undemocratic and manipulative systems without full consideration of its consequences in the public sphere (see also Adler, 2017; Cadwalladr, 2018). Normative expectations of critical scholars participating in solution-making is one I very much understand, and often agree with, certainly where we take up such activities as invited, ethical forms of pitching in (Paradise & Rogoff, 2009) in the communities we work with. However, I have also become worried that demands for solution-making are increasingly taking ideological forms as assumedly inherent or unassailably universal. Without rejecting the ethical value in research(ers) participating in solution-making, this chapter explores research presented as solutionless participation, and it considers what value drawing one another into dissatisfying impasses or dilemmas may have for developing habits of stalling solution-making as both an ethical and analytic method.

Over the last four years, I have considered the value and potential forms that writing about research for critical interaction may take (e.g., Vernon, 2016), and I have found that presentations of solutionless or purposefully complexifying narratives are often met with resistance because they do not align with the structural and performative expectations of conclusivity among colleagues. As but one brief example, I was only earlier this year delivering a paper at a conference when, just before I took to the lectern, a senior and established scholar in the field of education preemptively admonished my purposefully and deliberatively solutionless paper: If you tear a wall down, you must build a new one up. This expectation that I couple critique with solution-making was repeated afterward by a graduate student under this person's guidance, and this—among many other similar interactions with peers and colleagues in the various research communities of which I am a member—is the impetus for the following chapter. In these troubled times, I wonder what space and usefulness there may be for research—or, perhaps really, (re)presenting research—in projects of solutionless participation and if and how we can imagine solutionlessness and inconclusivity as appropriate entrance and dwelling spaces for foregrounding complex perspective-taking and collective response through critical scholarship.

I am not setting off on untrodden terrain, of course, although I hope to examine the topic of solution-making and solutionless participation from a unique vantage point and with perhaps somewhat novel logics. I will not be making a case for research as critique for the sake of critique, as if I were advocating academic and social arsonry, nor a case for abandoning solution-making on nihilistic or partisan grounds (see also Dennis, publishing as Korth, 2005). This will also not be a dismissal or disavowal of research as participation in solution-making, and I hope what follows will not be read as bent toward goals of silencing or devaluing such participation. It is not my intention to advocate closing off access to or diminishing the importance of solution-making. Instead I want to hold open space for research drawn into impasse, or sitting with inadequacy or inability, or solutionlessness as a potentially valuable state in which to dwell (such as solutionlessness as a call to collective response and transdisciplinarity, or to call to attention solution-making as an appendage of the overdetermining movements of Whiteness even within the constantly methodologized ethics of interaction; see also Povinelli, 2011) without fear of being chastised.

I hope, then, to invite readers into a critical interaction with a set of ideas: that demands of responsibility, rather than openness to the possibility, for researchers to participate in solution-making may at least (a) set the conditions for us to develop habits of misrecognizing and underestimating the problems we face; (b) falsely frame researchers and research projects as totalities, devaluing and setting unnecessary obstacles to collective action and sustained transdisciplinary, multigenerational effort; and (c) discourage—indeed, even make hard to imagine—research as sitting in and among problems, not idly or from a privileged inconsequential distance, but as implicated and called to account, as a call to pause and to call others—particularly those in positions of power—to pause when and where solution-making will become a deeply problematic and reifying project (see also Berlant, 2011), and where the seeming discomfort of solutionlessness may be a necessary practice of decolonization, of decentering one's claim as inherently necessary participant (see also Miller, 2018).

For the remainder of this chapter, I will draw on a research project that some wonderful colleagues and I have been working on within the University of Wisconsin system. Our ethnographic study serving as primary data was made possible with funding from the WT Grant Foundation and the Lumina Foundation. We were engaged in a two-year, comparative, multisited ethnography on four college campuses, designed to help us better understand how these campuses conceptualized and enacted college affordability. In turn, we learned how low- and middle-income first-year students on these campuses experienced, made sense of, and acted on their perceptions of the explicated and hidden costs of higher education. Thus, unlike the more common economistic approaches to understanding and measuring affordability (Molesworth, Scullion, & Nixon, 2010), our research was designed to map and deeply engage with students' meaning-making concerning what they hoped college would be and what it would accomplish, and whether it was therefore worth pursuing—that is, whether it is affordable within the contexts of their lives and histories.

We began our work together in August 2014. Logistically, we comprised five ethnographers from a variety of social science backgrounds embedded on four distinct campuses within the University of Wisconsin system. The four campuses were selected to address a number of hypotheses and assumptions in existing higher education literature on affordability. We selected schools that allowed for campus cross-comparisons of location, size, selectivity, average sticker price for low- and middle-income students, campus "climates" (a term I loathe, but that is for another time and place), and the political orientations of the communities in which the campuses were located. The entirety of the project included five months foregrounding institutional ethnographies on each campus, followed by 12 months of relational ethnographies with 12 to 15 first-year students on each campus. Students were followed from the start of the second semester of their first year in college to what might have been—if they continued—the end of the first semester of their second year. We remained on the campuses we were studying through the end of the second academic year, although with reduced interaction with students, faculty, and staff as we began to prioritize analyses and writing.

Because we came together from a variety of scholarly communities and histories of ethnographic research, attention was given from the start to developing a collaborative, comparative team that could work in parallel across research sites and settings. Our research design attempted to deepen our understanding and analyses of students' experiences of college affordability through a form of largely remote but consistent comparison, achieved through our convened trainings marked by joint generation of research themes and questions, weekly teleconferenced meetings preceded by written memos, and occasional visits to the various other campuses among the ethnographers involved in the study so that we could see one another's focal spaces.

Thus, our use of team-based ethnography is similar to, yet distinct from, more common approaches with longevity in qualitative research communities. Certainly most common is a form of team ethnography meant to open up the multivisibility of a research setting by situating more than one ethnographer among the field of study (e.g., Erikson & Stull, 1998). Within this form of team ethnography, researchers' meaning-making activities are dialogued in manners meant to add nuance and complexity to an explication of what became knowable (although not without problems; see Gerstl-Pepin & Gunzenhauser, 2002). Similarly, Whitt and Kuh (1991) describe the early use of a multisited, team-based approach to qualitative research while leaping, in small groups, from site to site across both space and time or as a serendipitous analytic partnership (e.g., Holyfield & Jonas, 2003; Woods, Boyle, Jeffrey, & Troman, 2000).

Instead, we attempted from the outset to negotiate what we refer to as comparative, parallel team ethnography. The four campuses, our research activities on them, and our team structure existed simultaneously, requiring us to carry out our research as brokers (Wenger, 1999) negotiating our straddled multimembership. In this way, we drew on the strengths of multisited, comparative research while expanding on the common uses of team ethnography, made possible primarily through recent advances in communicative technology. During our team research activities, we engaged in increasingly complex methods of intelligence (see also Stengel, 2001) as our interactions as a team and as ethnographers likewise grew more complex.

Due to the purposeful transdisciplinarity of our work and the capacity for unpredictable complexification always possible in ethnographic research projects (Carspecken, 1996), and the expansive potential in intersecting multiple institutions and activity systems (Engeström, 2001), solutionlessness became a frequent experience as we traced the multiplexity of systemic, socioeconomic, political, personal, and cultural aspects that shaped participants' experiences and knowledges. Although in past research I would consider this phase as en route to practical conclusivity, our work destabilized this assumption of typical research progress, and ongoing interactions with the academic communities of which I am a member highlighted how difficult it can be to then present solutionless critical research during a time when calls of research-as-action-as-solution-making hold privileged space.

I have been surprised to recently read more established, more intelligent critical writers devote their energies to justifying or advocating for value in research as solutionless participation (e.g., Coates, 2017; Povinelli, 2011; Roitman, 2014). Participation in solution-making (already a long-standing practice among some academic circles while denied others; see also Mirowski, 2014) is flourishing among social scientists and others in academia, breathing new life into unabashedly life-building projects such as scholar-activism (e.g., Suzuki & Mayorga, 2014) and community-based or participatory action research. To be a critical scholar not participating in solution-making, even if a temporary and deliberate action, demands explanation from our peers (e.g., Coates, 2017).

Coates's (2017) comparison of demanding solution-making as an obliged partner to critique as analogous to preventing a medical researcher from identifying a disease unless she is able to simultaneously offer a course of treatment is well put and worth expanding. I briefly held a faculty position in an elite, research-intensive medical school. I say "briefly" because it did not take long for me to realize the grave mismatch in our relationship and begin to seek opportunities to relocate to a more tenable academic environment. My time there did, however, provide access to new languages and logics that were not part of my repertoire of practice (Lave & Wenger, 1991) as someone from the social sciences, and Coates speaks directly to this. If I were to approach my medical colleagues at a conference with such a demand for solution-making as has been made of me at conferences and by journal reviewers, my claim would be destabilized as at best naive and at worst a disservice. Sometimes identifying and raising awareness of harms is the beginning of a sustained exploration of said harms and their weavings throughout a system, not the injection of remedy, and we should not wait to identify until an indeterminate point in time when we are ready to solution-make or arrive at a conclusion. At the risk of coming across as overly pithy, the social harms and injustices that social scientists address are no less complex than (and in some cases are more, and set the conditions for) the research focuses of my medical colleagues.

What follows, then, is an illustrative narrative drawn from this research. Although my colleagues and I had entered into our project focusing on higher education affordabilities, we quickly learned that, on the campus in which I was embedded, sexed and gendered injustices and violences were the experiences that constituted the meaning-making of many of the people with whom I worked and, in turn, many students' understandings of the tenability of college-going. Multiple entrance points for solution-making were complicated as we deepened our understanding of likely reentrenching or opening new forms of harm through taking part in solution-making, or were made inadequate as we traced the structural and systemic conditions and imaginings of college-going overdetermining institutional responses. Likewise, it became clear that identifying injustice and harm prior to, or even separate from, participating in solution-making was of paramount concern and unique value, benefiting multiple, valuable solutionless responses: (a) working with members of the community to uncover the shared and interdependent natures of injustices without tying success with rectifying response; (b) addressing multiple diverse academic communities through conferences as a form of scholarly ally-building toward collective action; (c) purposefully opening, rather than bounding off, our research so as to open it to expansive, transdisciplinary analyses; and (d) encouraging central and powerful members of the community—ourselves included—to engage with traumatic experiences through pausing, listening, and closing off our own potential escape routes under the deluding guise of solution-making.

None of this precludes the potential value in participating in solution-making, but it adds nuance by complicating how solution-making was understood and taken up and, I hope, provides students and junior scholars with some language for engaging with demands for specific participative performances in research communities that place obstacles on deliberative movements in our projects during times when solution-making seems unassailably inherent but may be counterproductive for justice. Likewise, I hope the following narrative serves as an entrance point, however partial, to engaging with critical ethnographic research not as a conclusive statement of knowledge but as an invitation to an expansive dilemma. In our troubled times—as if any times were not—I wonder whether research can be valuable as dissatisfying and lacking conclusivity, as an encounter with precariousness, an impasse that encourages methods of perspective-taking and imaging responses out to retrievable ends (Dewey, 1938), where solution-making is decoupled but not distant from critique as a process of inviting diverse, collective, multigenerational effort beyond any one research project's capacity.

Galena State University

In the fall of 2015, Galena State University (GSU) released its annual Security and Fire Safety Report, declaring that three instances of sexual assault had occurred during the 2014-2015 academic year. This number directly contradicted a student survey produced within the office of the Dean of Students indicating that GSU had one of the highest reported rates of sexual assault in the University of Wisconsin system. It also conflicted with my own ethnographic data: Of the 12 first-year, female-identified focal students with whom I worked, two reported violent sexual assaults, each was able to identify a friend or an acquaintance who was assaulted at GSU, and every female student could describe near-daily examples of sexual harassment.

Located in a rural, White, politically conservative part of Wisconsin, GSU identifies itself as a science, technology, engineering, and mathematics (STEM)–focused, four-year university that takes prides in its low sticker price and being a good "bang for your buck." Over the course of the research, it became increasingly evident how deeply sexism and misogyny shaped GSU's campus culture compared with the other campuses in our team ethnography. For example, two other campus's cultural norms and practices were similarly shaped by systematized racism and xenophobia. Both of these campuses responded by creating well-resourced support services, physical spaces designed to be controlled by minoritized students and their allies, and campus-wide plans purportedly designed to support racially and ethnically minoritized students on campus. Minoritized students did not usually experience these responses as effective, nor did the responses significantly impact (or attempt to impact) White students' experiences on campus, save in ways that increased their comfort (see also Leonardo & Porter, 2010; Vernon, 2014). Therefore, institutional responses did not end or even always lessen minoritized students' experiences of harassment. They did, however, provide a framework, a structure, and resources for minoritized students to gather, share their experiences, and push for organizational change. Students who participated in these structures recognized and demanded that the university organize a more appropriate and ethical systemic response to a systemic problem. Although the universities' responses were fraught, often ineffective, and largely limited to students participating in racially segregated programs, the universities did take action and provide resources to address students' concerns, even if only to publicly represent themselves as inclusive spaces.

In contrast to these other campuses within the University of Wisconsin system, GSU did not publicly acknowledge the severity and depth of gendered and sexed inequities on campus, did not respond to these issues systematically (e.g., through initiatives, support services, or special programs), and did not make space for students or staff to lead or participate in a campus response. Instead, campus administrators made policy decisions that tended to dismiss rather than recognize students' college attendance as one of physical and social danger.

GSU's institutionalized sexism was evident in many different arenas. For example, GSU regularly misrepresented data related to gender and sexuality on campus. Privileging their official police data on sexual assault over large-scale, nationally representative student surveys was one example of this pattern. So was their representation of gendered student ratios on campus. Guides on campus tours were taught to assuage public concerns about a gendered imbalance by cheering the fact that "there are more female students than ever" enrolled. Although this fact is numerically true because of overall trends in student enrollment, in actuality, the gender gap on campus had been steadily widening for the better half of a decade. The gap hit a five-year high in the 2015-2016 academic year, when female-identified students accounted for only about 30% of new enrollees. In other words, although, yes, there were "more female students than ever" on campus, there were also more male-identified students than ever and at higher rates of enrollment.

GSU also refused to conduct or respond to gendered analyses of its academic, recreational, or residential programs or policies. The mathematics department had a history of using math placement exam scores as a gatekeeper to STEM majors and disproportionately placed female-identified students in remedial math courses at rates well above the national average (see Sparks & Malkus, 2013). These courses increased female-identified students' costs and time to completion (because they did not earn credit hours for taking such courses) and overdetermined female students' academic pathways. "We're in remedial math; we don't get to be engineers," focal student Arya pointed out to a peer when hearing her talk about her intended major. Presented with these data, administrators said they had no idea that female students were disproportionately and significantly more likely to be placed in remedial math than their male peers—they had tracked racially minoritized students but not gendered disparities. The campus response to these data was to largely but quietly double-down on its initiatives: over the course of one year, blocking my access to data from the office of institutional research, defunding its remedial math tutoring center, and managerializing a stringent tracking system to auto-enroll students into these courses while limiting students' credit hours and ultimately expelling students who were not completing remedial math requirements during the first two years of enrolling at GSU.

However, it was not just that GSU's academic systems consistently favored male-identified members of the campus community. In addition, female students at GSU were regularly and publicly subjected to sexual harassment and violence. Those who wished to use the campus's recreation facilities explained that they had to avoid peak "male hours," such as when an athletic team was using the spaces—not due to a lack of space but because of the harassment. Those students with the funds to do so purchased private memberships at off-campus facilities—just one other example of "the pink tax" students pointed out they paid to attend GSU. Male students commonly catcalled at women who were walking through campus or in residence halls, a group of students living off-campus put up a plywood sign that read "Thank you for your daughters" on a main street during the 2014 new student move-in day, and multiple students described male students in residence halls following their bodies with laser pointers when they walked at night through campus. Lizzie, for example, regularly had to walk at night on an unlit path in the woods from a cluster of residence halls to the main dining facility—the only place on campus where students could get a full meal for a reasonable price. One night, around 9 p.m., "all of a sudden I see a green laser being flashed on me. It was on my back, but sometimes they'd miss and it'd hit my hand or something, so I'd see it." She pretended to be on her phone, but she could hear a group of male students calling at her from a window in the residence hall somewhere behind her. She had gotten through the woods quite far when suddenly the green laser was back on her—coming from somewhere in the woods around her. The experience of having a laser pointer trained on one's body while walking from dinner was a clear reminder that female bodies were viewed as open targets, bodies to be hunted. The lack of any administrative response to complaints—even a response as simple as lighting the path through the woods or sending out a condemning e-mail—was a clear reminder that the institution seemed to tacitly support, or at least certainly not condemn, such violence.

Female administrators and staff had their own stories to tell. One vice chancellor, out for a morning jog on new student move-in day, found herself being judged by a group of male students acting as if they were at a gymnastics or diving competition and "ranking" with numbered scorecards the physical performance of any female whose pathway crossed in front of their porch. She laughed, telling me something like that is always going on. Another full-time staff member explained that when she was an undergraduate student at GSU, she felt perfectly comfortable moving through the town at night, but she refused to walk alone through campus. Instead, she would request a campus security officer to walk with her. "I figured I was just overreacting; being irrational. It never occurred to me that other women were unsafe here." This feeling that the harassment experience was innocuous or individualized and irrational was common across research participants; the vice chancellor seeming to brush off what she thought was an immature, boyish culture, and Lizzy, echoing the staff member, said, "I thought I was alone in dealing with sexual harassment. I thought I was the only one."

Each woman's sense that she was the only one was overdetermined through the administration's response to the widespread gender and sexual harassment that permeated campus. For example, after spending the better part of the 2014-2015 academic year surveying students' experiences with and attitudes toward sexual harassment and violence, a staff member from the dean's office published a damning report of student attitudes and institutional responses. She gave an advertised, public presentation to the university community. Eight people attended, none of them students, and none upper-level administrators. She gave a second presentation a few days later and was able to get better attendance, in part, because a class on the sociology of gender attended for participation credit. However, she was told that she could not form a task force on sexual harassment, and that the university would not systematically address the results of the study. Frustrated, she soon left GSU to work with a local advocacy group.

Rachel, a high-achieving student on a full academic scholarship, was a member of an invitation-only student leadership team meant to be paragons of the campus community. Among many of the expected roles and perks with her status came periodic dinners hosted by GSU's chancellor. During her third year as a student, she found herself sitting next to him and took the opportunity to ask what he and the university intended to do about the issues female-identified students were having on campus. She remembered vividly how he turned to her and responded, "We do enough for them already," and then returned to his conversation with one of her male peers to talk about the most recent football game.

The Center for Gender and Sexuality similarly struggled to call the administration to action and was chastised for its efforts during our study. Throughout the winter and spring of 2016, someone(s) had been moving through campus at night, stripping "safe zone" placards—denoting that occupants had completed training with the center and were actively welcoming and working to make the university a space for LGBTQA members—off doors and windows. The director of the center fielded new e-mails of stolen placards every day for several months, while she in turn fought for a campus-wide, administrative response, including drafting a letter for the chancellor to send to the campus (no one but the chancellor could send out university e-mails). What the community received after almost three months of requests from the center was trivializing; an e-mail to the campus entrenching otheredness of the LGBTQA community with calls for tolerance for the sake of feeling safe rather than acknowledging the unsafe realities of attempting to live within GSU. Campus police launched a lighthearted initiative on campus social media, stating that it had placed invisible theft detection powder on some placards, and encouraged students to "Show us your hands!" and "High-five for diversity!" in photographs uploaded to campus media accounts. The university had shifted its attention elsewhere after two or three days.

But for LGBTQA students, attention to safety was a constant life reality. Huck entered GSU while transitioning, socially and financially estranged from his family and understanding GSU's on-campus residences would be violently unsafe for him. The university requires both first- and second-year students to live on campus save for particular nontraditional student conditions, such as age and marital status or commuting from a guardian's home. Huck fit no excusable conditions, and his familial estrangement left him without the financial resources to pay for a single room on campus, and thus he was left in a precarious situation. He found a tenable but unlawful solution in camouflaging his housing, telling the university he was commuting from his mother's house while telling his family he was living on campus, all the while renting a room in a house occupied by LGBTQA members of the local community. It made college attendance financially and socially viable, but he was under the constant threat of discovery and expulsion—or an increased financial burden tantamount to expulsion—during his first two years of college.

Female-identified and nonmasculine, nonheteronormative students' lives were radically transformed by attending GSU. For many, the constant harassment, fear for their safety, and regularized messages that they were second-class people and students resulted in increasing isolation and other emotional, academic, psychological, and physical costs. Many decided to transfer. Indeed, GSU had the highest transfer rate of all the universities in the study. Those students who decided to stay often paid a steep personal price. Lizzy came to GSU from a large city in Wisconsin primarily because she was looking for a White, conservative community. She turned down acceptances to attend multiple other public and private institutions in the state. Lizzy described her high school as "ghetto . . . a majority is a mix of the minorities. So Blacks, Latinos, and all that, and then the Whites." She thought of herself as a White conservative, and she saw diversity as creating more problems than it solved. GSU seemed like a place where she could find like-minded people: "I was just sick of the city, I guess. So I decided to come here."

Lizzy reflected on her decision and its antecedents: "I was a stupid 17-year-old. I loved it at first, but meeting the people here . . . the racism and sexism; I'm a lot more liberal than I thought I was!" Lizzy and her roommate—born in China but adopted as a baby by White parents and raised in Wisconsin—initially befriended a group of seven male-identified students in their residence hall. This strategy was common: Female-identified students found it difficult to maintain friendships or access to social spaces without joining a predominantly male-identified group, but they paid a steep price for this access.

"They would always crack Chinese or Asian jokes at her, like 'You eat dog' or 'Your skin is yellow!', and then laugh. You could tell it bothered her, and sometimes they'd stop for a week or so, but they'd always come back to it. And then they would . . . they love . . . they love Black jokes."

The group also regularly made sexist jokes or sexual innuendos toward her and her roommate; the instructor for her psychology class encouraged her to record her conversations and edit them down to a clip for class. Lizzie cut a single, 17-minute interaction down to five minutes; she described the recording as "Seven different sexual comments toward me, and then a couple of 'woman jokes' thrown in there, too."

Her relationship with these men in her residence hall meant access to alcohol and parties, but when they started pushing her to drink when she didn't want to and made sexual advances despite having girlfriends, she began to hang out with them less and less. Then one day, Lizzy and her roommate wondered aloud, in front of the seven male students, why they were always harassed: the whistling while walking to class, the laser pointers, the sexual innuendos and sexist jokes.

"One of the guys said, 'It's because you're girls.' And another, who is in my psychology of women class—he calls it his culinary class—says it's because we need to put women down to maintain the status quo. But this other guy says it's because he's the superior gender. But the way he said it; like, the tone of his voice . . . he meant it. Oh my god, that's how they think."

Lizzy was double-majoring in criminal justice and psychology, and she had begun to think about transferring to another university with a larger and more diverse population. She visited a friend at a campus in one of the state's cities and immediately liked the campus; they went to a house party, and she found it much more enjoyable than parties at GSU. She began seriously considering a transfer, and then during the winter of her first year at GSU, Lizzy was sexually assaulted in the residence hall by someone she had considered a friend. She had invited him over one night to talk; she had been having a difficult week as she fell out of friendship groups and wanted to talk to someone. "He had tried stuff before, but I always said no—I really like to hang out with you, but you have to stop." When he got to her dorm room, she explicitly told him "not to try anything funny" because she had come to expect unwanted advances. She remembered him saying, "Yeah, I'm not going to." Soon he began trying to kiss her, but she "pushed him away . . . I was in a bad mood, and I was not going to give in." But he grabbed her, holding her down on her own bed. "I kept telling him to stop, and he wouldn't—I should have kicked him out then, but he's my friend, and he's a fun guy to be around, and I finally said, 'Fine, I'll kiss you, but this is the last time." But he pinned her down, and, "I . . . just gave in, and it happened. Eventually I pushed him off of me, and started crying."

He apologized, telling her she hadn't done anything wrong, but as soon as she stopped crying, "He grabbed me and started doing it again. He said, 'It's already happened once, what's the difference if it happens again?'"

He convinced her not to report the assault to the university, and for a while she kept her trauma to herself. But she saw a mental health counselor who encouraged her to come forward. The final project for her second-semester English class was a research paper, and one of the other female students in class, Faith, had written and presented a paper on sexual assault on college campuses, opening up to the class about her own experience during her first year at GSU. Faith was a model of bravery to Lizzy, and so Lizzy went to the dean of students with her story.

When Faith went to GSU to study criminal justice, she was a nontraditional student, already in her mid-20s and a single parent with a child in kindergarten. She had spent two years at a technical college and transferred to finish her degree in three years. She and her son were living below the poverty line, surviving on student aid and tax returns while she was in school. Faith had a childhood of abuse and suffered from posttraumatic stress disorder (PTSD); she often contemplated suicide and had spent a long weekend during the fall of that first semester in a psychiatric facility after an attempt to kill herself. When she was having a difficult day or she didn't trust herself to stay alive until morning, she would have friends stay with her through the night to make sure "nothing happened."

Faith worked as a part-time housekeeper and caretaker at a live-in facility for adults with disabilities. The job was almost an hour away by car; the area around GSU had no public bus system. The income from her work was just enough to cover gas, utility bills, and some food; tax returns, coupled with financial aid, covered the rest. When Faith was able to get a bit of money together, she would pay rent forward as far as she could so that her son would have a place to live, "just in case." She refused makeup and dressed each day in the same knit hat and oversized sweatpants and sweatshirt, telling friends who asked why she never altered her appearance that she had a kid and didn't have the time or money to care about looks. Standing at five feet, 10 inches, she came across as strong and intimidating, but she described herself as physically weak; she was, she said, angry but not violent.

Her son's biological father lived nearby with his girlfriend, and her son visited him every other week. She suspected the girlfriend of abuse, and when he came back from these visits, she would take photographs of new bruises on his arms and take notes on fearful reactions, such as undressing him for a bath or bed. He was seeing a therapist, and she was hoping these conversations would shed light on what was going on and help in her custody battle.

A few weeks into her first semester at GSU, Faith had a weekend to herself while her son was visiting his father, and so she decided to go out to the bars with a friend. Having the night to herself was a rare occasion; she drank hard as they hopped from bar to bar—hard enough that, around 1 a.m. in the morning, she "couldn't see straight" and could not remember where she lived or how to get there. A male friend offered to walk her home, but he led her against her protests behind a garden shed in a neighborhood yard, where he forced her to perform oral sex. After a few minutes, Faith was able to get herself off the ground and tried to run away; he "grabbed [her] from behind, like in a bear-hug," but she broke free and ran. She doesn't remember how or by when, but she found her way home and fell into bed.

The next day, she immediately texted the man who had assaulted her and tried to get him to confess; he told her that he had gone back to the bars and drank until he blacked out, so he couldn't remember anything from the night before. Not believing him, she went to both the local police and GSU administrators, trying to get some form of recognition and response. After that point, Faith's first year at GSU was consumed with meetings. She would regularly meet with the police department to try and push her case forward, and she went from GSU administrator to administrator, trying to find someone to take up her case against the male student who had assaulted her. Among work, parenting, the costs of being poor, and the legal and bureaucratic struggles of moving her assault case forward, she had limited time for school. Twice, she needed to drop a required course—not because it was difficult but because she could not organize her schedule to be able to consistently arrive on time.

Her meetings with both police and administrators were ongoing deadends. There was alcohol involved, and the man consistently denied being part of the assault. Officials frequently pointed out that there were no signs of physical trauma in the forms of bruises, scratches, or ripped hair, and so she was pushed into two alternate explanations: regret after the fact, or she had the wrong guy. But Faith knew what she knew, most of the time, and came to resent GSU's administration for responding as they did. In particular, she signaled out the dean of students and the chancellor. She felt the former listened to her with no intention of helping, whereas the latter actively questioned her like a defense lawyer, trying to poke holes in her story or make her question her experience.

Heading into her second year, Faith sought out other female students who had suffered sexual assault at GSU. She had considered transferring away, but she didn't want the school to have the satisfaction of stripping her of her ability to finish her degree. She had known financial and familial precarity and depression for much of her life, and her primary response to this traumatic event, as with other events in her life, was anger and an unwillingness to give in or give up. She tried to form a support group on campus for survivors of sexual assault, and she met other students with similar experiences. Unfortunately, they found it difficult to effectively advertise on campus because the administration showed no willingness to get the word out or open meeting space even after they became an official student group, and it appeared to be a short-lived attempt at community-building. At the same time, Faith's PTSD was taking its toll, and a series of car troubles sapped her finances heading into the winter months. Faith had been visiting aid agencies, but they told her they couldn't help until she had an eviction notice or been evicted and was homeless—exactly the outcomes she was trying to avoid as the cold winter months approached. Her mother finally offered to pay a month's rent as long as Faith paid her back when she could. That helped in the short run, but Faith explained, "I haven't been to counseling in a while, just while trying to deal with everything else. It cuts into the time; it's like I'm stressed out all the time, but my PTSD has been bad lately—a lot of flashbacks, and nightmares. Especially at night . . . I can't even—I don't know how to describe it. It's like this never-ending cycle of blackness."

Faith had to drop another class heading into winter; she owed the university just under $2,000 from the previous semester. She negotiated with the financial aid office and registrar to dip into her upcoming aid. She got a couple of space heaters in case she had to choose between gas or electricity bills during the Wisconsin winter.

Going into what she hoped was her last semester, Faith's attempts to be vocal about sexual assault on the GSU campus were shifting in response to her own increasingly precarious relationship to the university and seemingly impermeable institutional structures.

"Seeing on social media that girls have been raped on campus. And there's this one girl [who is also striving to be active in women's advocacy], she tells people not to report it to the university, because nothing's going to come of it. And I kind of tell people that [now], too; I say 'you can do what you want, but it's not really worth it, in my opinion.'"

Lizzy had gone to the dean of students, at Faith's recommendation, at the end of her first year. She thought the dean was wonderful—she listened, empathized, and seemed genuinely concerned for Lizzy's well-being. However, Lizzy also got the clear impression that her trauma was hers to deal with—the dean was there to listen, but the institution would not act. Over the summer before her second year, Lizzy began to suffer from depression and anxiety. She considered not returning for her second year, but in the end, she decided to try one more time. Three weeks in, she hadn't been able to leave her bed in her residence hall; the depression and anxiety had taken over, and she couldn't get herself out of bed for much more than the bathroom or food. Distraught, she called her parents to pick her up and withdrew from GSU. Lizzy returned to her parents' house, taking a job as a bartender while she saw a psychologist and tried to work out how to reclaim her life.

"I mean, there's a lot of talk these days about 'climate' on campus," the chancellor said with an undertone of exasperation, "and I think it's important. You have to work on that. But fundamentally, what I want our students to know is [that] I want them to get degrees. Maybe I can change this place's climate so that it's all warm and fuzzy. I don't think I can, but we'll try that. But at the end of the day, they need to go to class, they need to do the schoolwork. And we are to support them in their academic achievement. And you know what? They start achieving academically. It's amazing how some of those other things become less important."

Prologue

Contrary to accessible U.S. imaginations of collegiate activity, students at GSU did not gather for collective response. They did not protest. Nothing. During my two years on campus, while the rest of Wisconsin reacted to a wholesale remaking and rapid defunding of the state's university system, GSU stayed strangely, purposefully silent. "It's this great bubble outside of politics and everything out there," a male-identified student gushed when explaining how he perceived the campus, and therefore the normative relationships students, faculty, and staff were joined in. The nail that stands out gets pounded down; clear passage would be given to those who stayed in formation. The fact that the system routinely fucks over students makes this arrangement untenable and unjust; GSU is unaffordable and denies affordances for nonmajoritarian members.

Ethnography is made up of both tangible and intangible knowledges; absent or only alluded to in the previous explication of GSU are the political, economic, and historical trajectories within which the campus and its activities are further elucidated; additional forms of data open or widen entrances, but anything short of a book sweeps into the corner of the cutting room. Instead, I have purposefully foregrounded the aesthetic and atmospheric experience of the inescapable and suffocatingly specious neutrality of GSU culture that double-binds nonmajoritarian members of the community to unjust forms of endurance and academic death. I am also purposefully avoiding solution-making and conclusivity in this particular rendition of our work to potentiate the alternative critical interactions closed off or severely bracketed when assenting to empirical traditions of finality.

What, then, of research as solutionless participation and representation as denying conclusivity? Data analysis may be understood as developing habits of stalling ourselves with a hermeneutics of suspicion (Leonardo & Porter, 2010) of our subtle and culturally conditioned movements toward meaning-making. Demands for empirical representations of solution-making and claims of finality or conclusivity are also, I think, worth stalling and approaching with an empathetic suspicion because it may be of value for research to invite into spaces and projects without providing clear exits—or even closing off exits, where those function as face-saving escape routes from identity threats to powered interests or beneficiaries. In other words, we may need to open multiple entrances to the spaces and places of harm and trauma that constitute the realities of our historical moment and keep these spaces difficult to not sit within the circulations of injustices. Without the built-in buoyancy of empirical solving or concluding, researchers have the opportunity to complicate our relationships with and within social projects, opening into the nearby and shared traumas of existence as a way of life within regimes of (at least) our current forms of majoritarianism, making possible new habits of intelligence toward collective ethical deliberation and earnest, empathetic suspicion of culturally conditioned solution-making.

References

Adler, S. (2017, July 27). Breaking news. *Radiolab*. Retrieved from https://radiolab.org
Berlant, L. (2011). *Cruel optimism*. Durham, NC: Duke University Press.
Cadwalladr, C. (2018, March 18). The Cambridge Analytica files. *The Guardian*. Retrieved from https://www.theguardian.com
Carspecken, P. (1996). *Critical ethnography in educational research: A theoretical and practical guide*. New York, NY: Routledge.
Coates, T. (2017). *We were eight years in power: An American tragedy*. New York, NY: One World.
Dewey, J. (1929). *Human nature and conduct: An introduction to social psychology*. New York, NY: Henry Holt & Co.
Dewey, J. (1938). *Experience and education*. New York, NY: Macmillan.
Engeström, Y. (2001). Expansive learning at work: Toward an activity theoretical reconceptualization. *Journal of Education and Work*, 14(1), 133-156.

Erikson, K., & Stull, D. (1998). *Doing team ethnography: Warnings and advice.* Thousand Oaks, CA: Sage.
Gerstl-Pepin, C. I., & Gunzenhauser, M. G. (2002). Collaborative team ethnography and the paradoxes of interpretation. *International Journal of Qualitative Studies in Education, 15*(2), 137-154.
Gutierrez, R. (2017, March 20). White folks and faux nihilism. *Silicon Valley De-Bug.* Retrieved from https://www.siliconvalleydebug.org
Holyfield, L., & Jonas, L. (2003). From river god to research grunt: Identity, emotions, and the river guide. *Symbolic Interaction, 26*(2), 285-306.
Kendall, N., Vernon, F., Goerisch, D., Kim, E., & Wolfgram, M. (2015, May 20-23). *Negotiating and managing a team ethnography across sites and settings.* Paper presented at the 11th International Congress of Qualitative Inquiry, Champaign-Urbana, IL.
Korth, B. (2005). Necessity, choice, or narcissism? A feminist does feminist ethnography. In G. Troman, B. Jeffery, & G. Walford (Eds.), *Methodological issues and practices in ethnography* (pp. 131-167). Bingley, UK: Emerald Group Publishing Limited.
Lave, J., & Wenger, E. (1991). *Situated learning: Legitimate peripheral participation.* Cambridge, UK: Cambridge University Press.
Leonardo, Z., & Porter, R. K. (2010). Pedagogies of fear: Toward a Faonian theory of "safety" in race dialog. *Race Ethnicity and Education, 13*(2), 139-157.
Miller, B. (2018, February 25). If you want to be an effective ally, be quiet and know your place. *The Huffington Post.* Retrieved from https://www.huffingtonpost.com
Mirowski, P. (2014). *Never let a serious crisis go to waste: How neoliberalism survived the financial meltdown.* Brooklyn, NY: Verso.
Molesworth, M., Scullion, R., & Nixon, E. (Eds.). (2010). *The marketisation of higher education and the student as consumer.* London, UK: Routledge.
Paradise, R., & Rogoff, B. (2009). Side by side: Learning by observing and pitching in. *Ethos, 37*(1), 102-138.
Povinelli, E. (2011). *Economies of abandonment: Social belonging and endurance in late liberalism.* Durham, NC: Duke University Press.
Rogoff, B., & Angelillo, C. (2002). Investigating the coordinated functioning of multifaceted cultural practices in human development. *Human Development, 45*(1), 211-225.
Roitman, J. (2014). *Anti-crisis.* Durham, NC: Duke University Press.
Sparks, D., & Malkus, N. (2013, January). First-year undergraduate remedial course-taking: 1999-2000, 2003-04, 2007-08. Statistics in Brief. NCES 2013-013. National Center for Education Statistics.
Stengel, B. S. (2001). Making use of the method of intelligence. *Educational Theory, 51*(1), 109-125.
Suzuki, D., & Mayorga, E. (2014). Scholar-activism: A twice-told tale. *Multicultural Perspectives, 16*(1), 16-20.

Vernon, F. (2014). The paradox of structured autonomy: A critical ethnography of challenge-by-choice and safe spaces in adventure-based experiential education. *Other Education: The Journal of Educational Alternatives, 3*(2), 22-44.

Vernon, F. (2016). The diversity project: An ethnography of social justice and experiential education programming. *Ethnography and Education, 11*(3), 298-315.

Wenger, E. (1999). *Communities of practice: Learning, meaning, and identity.* Cambridge, UK: Cambridge University Press.

Whitt, E. J., & Kuh, G. D. (1991). Qualitative methods in a team approach to multiple-institution studies. *The Review of Higher Education, 14*(3), 317-337.

Woods, P., Boyle, M., Jeffrey, B., & Troman, G. (2000). A research team in ethnography. *International Journal of Qualitative Studies in Education, 13*(1), 85-98.

Yancy, G. (Ed.). (2004). *What White looks like: African-American philosophers on the Whiteness question.* New York, NY: Routledge.

CHAPTER 5

Their Own Ways of Knowing
Art-Based Participatory Action Research with Refugee Women from Burma

Hillary Rubesin and Madison Hayes

> *I want to make sure we do something. I want this to be important. I will participate in research if we move it to the next level.*
> —REFUGEE WOMAN FROM BURMA, DEBATING RESEARCH PARTICIPATION

REFUGEE WOMEN PRESENT a unique subset of the more than 65 million displaced people in the world. Although these women often struggle with complex trauma, their issues can go unvoiced and unaddressed in the midst of shifting landscapes, gender roles, and cultural norms. This chapter uses a case study approach to depict an art-based participatory action research project conducted with a small group of refugee women from Burma resettled in Orange County, North Carolina. Group facilitators and researchers came from both a community-based agency as well as a local university. Issues stemming from this institutional partnership are addressed throughout the chapter, especially as they relate to how the partnership impacted the refugee women and their stated research goals.

Through the four-month data-collection process, the importance of the Women's Group was discovered and solidified. Participants employed art-based participatory action research processes to explore issues of importance to them and to achieve their ultimate goal of making the Women's Group strong and stable. Cultural humility and cultural safety on the part of the facilitators played an integral part in the research process. These concepts are explored at the end of the chapter in an effort to challenge hierarchical research paradigms, as well as to deconstruct traditional ideas of "legitimate" knowledge.

Who We Are / What We Do

First, to situate ourselves, we are both White, cis, able-bodied, American-born, salaried, young leaders of two community-based nonprofit organizations that work almost exclusively within disenfranchised communities of color. Our identities inform, complicate, and shape the work we do every day. We write from positions of privilege and feel it is important to name that from the start.

Hillary is the executive director of the Art Therapy Institute (ATI; www.ncati.org), a Carrboro, North Carolina–based organization of mental health professionals dedicated to the healing power of the arts. ATI provides expressive therapies services to more than 500 clients from diverse backgrounds annually. In addition to these clinical services, ATI leads education and advocacy efforts across the state and strives to conduct ethical, culturally congruent research.

One of ATI's largest clinical programs, the Newcomer Art Therapy Project (NATP; http://www.ncati.org/the-newcomer-art-therapy-project), currently serves more than 200 refugees and immigrants from more than 25 countries worldwide. This program is conducted within multiple settings, such as schools, health clinics, homes, and other community-based spaces, to "meet clients where they are." Art therapy, a mental health field that incorporates arts-based practices within the psychotherapeutic relationship (American Art Therapy Association, 2017), is especially effective when working with refugees because it has the ability to transcend language and cultural barriers, both contain and evoke complex emotions, process traumatic memories through visual representations, inspire new ways of thinking, and re-create a sense of home for displaced people (Dieterich-Hartwell & Koch, 2017).

Madison directs the Refugee Community Partnership (RCP; https://refugeecommunitypartnership.org/), a refugee community–driven organization, also located in Carrboro–Chapel Hill, a region with some of the worst economic and health disparities in North Carolina. RCP mobilizes local residents, organizations, agencies, schools, and businesses into a powerful, cross-sector support infrastructure for refugee residents. By creating culturally appropriate pathways to local opportunities and resources, and forging relationships between those who can navigate and access institutions and those who cannot, RCP sustains the lifelong process of rebuilding home.

In 2017, the ATI and the RCP joined forces to strengthen and sustain a support group for local women resettled from Burma. This chapter details the activist research—designed and implemented by the refugee women from Burma themselves—that sparked this organizational partnership and enabled the continuity of a vital community service.

Refugee Resettlement and Mental Health

As of 2016, across the globe 65.3 million people have been forcibly displaced—the highest number in reported history (United Nations High Commissioner for Refugees, 2016). Human migration across international borders continues to grow, in major part, due to religious, ethnic, and political persecution; economic crises; natural disasters; and resource depletion (Crosby, 2013). On top of premigration and migration trauma, refugees often encounter numerous difficulties after resettling in host countries, including but not limited to barriers to housing, employment, health care, communication, and education, as well as antinewcomer sentiment in both personal interactions and public policies (Appel, 2012; Ellis, MacDonald, Lincoln, & Cabral, 2008; Millington, 2010; Morris, Popper, Rodwell, Brodine, & Brouwer, 2009; Newman, Hartman, & Taber, 2012; Pedersen & Thomas, 2013). Some researchers have suggested that these types of postmigration stressors negatively impact mental health more than premigration or migration trauma (Schweitzer, Brough, Vromans, & Asic-Kobe, 2011).

Refugee women are particularly susceptible to postmigration issues. Women are often responsible for holding their families together, and they must do so in the midst of shifting cultural norms and gender roles between their countries of origins and host communities (Connor et al., 2016; Koh, Liamputtong, & Walker, 2013). Compounding these issues, unfamiliar and often difficult changes to traditional family structures may trigger instances of or ongoing domestic abuse (Chantler, 2012; Norsworthy & Khuankaew, 2004).

Unfortunately, language and gender barriers often prevent refugee women from speaking out about resettlement difficulties and/or having healthy relationships with host community members (Clark, Gilbert, Rao, & Kerr, 2014; Watkins, Razee, & Richters, 2012). Participatory research approaches—especially those that incorporate the arts—may offer refugee women the opportunity to express themselves and process the issues they face as newcomers in effective, creative, accessible, therapeutic, and cross-cultural ways (Dieterich-Hartwell & Koch, 2017). These inclusive approaches honor the ability of participants to determine their own needs and priorities and empower them to take direct action to achieve their stated goals (Baird et al., 2015; Collie, Liu, Podsiadlowski, & Kindon, 2010; Gilhooly & Lynn, 2015; Guruge & Khanlou, 2004; Norsworthy & Khuankaew, 2004; Okigbo, Reierson, & Stowman, 2009).

Refugees in North Carolina

North Carolina, the ninth-most-populated state in the United States (U.S. Census Bureau, 2015), consistently falls within the top 10 states for refugee resettlement (Radford & Connor, 2016). Orange County, North Carolina (approximate population: 142,000), the area under study, has an estimated foreign-born population of 12.7% according to census information collected between 2012 and 2016 (U.S. Census Bureau, 2017).

Since 2007, the majority of refugees resettled to Orange County have been from Burma (Clifford, 2016; Pew Research Center, 2017). Those refugees arriving from Burma have descended from various ethnic groups, including Karen, Chin, Burmese (or Burman), and, most recently, Rohingya. These ethnic groups can be further divided by language and cultural differences—such as S'gaw Karen and Poe Karen—and by tensions carried over from years of civil unrest.

Many ethnic minorities (such as the Karen and Rohingya people, among others) have been systemically persecuted by the ruling Burmese regime since the early 1960s (Barron et al., 2007). Despite these histories of violent conflict as well as a multitude of cultural/lingual differences distinguishable among the ethnic groups, the diverse communities from Burma are often treated as one community on resettlement, increasing the possibility of postresettlement conflict and misunderstanding (Cathcart, Decker, Ellenson, & Amell, 2007).

Mental Health Services for Refugees in North Carolina

In 2007, a group of students from the University of North Carolina–Chapel Hill's Gillings School of Global Public Health conducted a needs assessment of the local refugee community from Burma and, among many issues, found a lack of accessible, culturally appropriate mental health options for refugees from Burma resettled in Orange County (Cathcart et al., 2007). One of the authors of this report expanded on these findings in her master's thesis, which advocated for art therapy as a potentially beneficial mental health approach for resettled refugee children from Burma (Ellenson, 2008). Ellenson highlighted that art therapy circumvents verbal language barriers, is approachable for various cultural communities, destigmatizes the treatment of mental illness, and allows for trauma to be processed visually, just as it is stored in the brain.

Based on the recommendations of the Ellenson (2008) report, in 2008, the ATI was awarded a $7,000 pilot grant from a local foundation to launch a weekly art therapy program for a small group of refugee adolescents from Burma in one self-contained public school classroom. ATI's NATP has since expanded to reach more than 200 refugee and immigrant children, adolescents, and adults annually across four counties in North Carolina. The program is currently stationed within 20 different schools, two community health centers, two resettlement agencies, and three other community-based programs focused on refugee support. Funding for NATP now stems from private donations, foundation grants, school contracts, county funding, and Medicaid billing, with a program budget of approximately $130,000 annually.

In 2013, two miles down the road from ATI, the University of North Carolina at Chapel Hill began the Refugee Mental Health and Wellness Initiative (RW; http://refugeewellness.web.unc.edu/history-of-refugee-wellness/) to help address the ongoing and underaddressed mental health needs of refugees within Orange, Wake, and Durham Counties of North Carolina. By providing clinical services for and research on local refugee communities, this initiative helped expand options for refugee mental health support. To date, ATI and RW are the only Orange County, NC–based programs with projects focused specifically on refugee mental health.

The Current Study

In 2016, ATI asked to collaborate with RW to facilitate an ongoing mental health and wellness group for refugee women from Burma. Both programs had been running separate women's groups for this population and determined it would be more effective and efficient to combine efforts instead of duplicating services. Master's-level social work students interning at RW agreed to facilitate Pathways to Wellness (PTW), an eight-session curriculum designed to address culture shock, the "refugee experience," mental health, mind-body connections, goals and dreams, and creating wellness and community (Pathways to Wellness, 2011). Staff members and master's-level interns from ATI agreed to incorporate self-designed, arts-based directives into the PTW curriculum in hopes of helping participants experience and integrate the information more effectively.

Although attendance shifted over the course of the PTW curriculum, 14 Burmese, Karen, and Rohingya women, ranging in age from their early 20s to late 70s, participated in the program. ATI was able to secure an experienced interpreter who spoke both Burmese and Karen to help facilitate the communication process and attempt to understand the refugee women's needs as fully as possible. Unfortunately, no in-person female Rohingya interpreters were found in the Chapel Hill–Carrboro area, and Rohingya phone interpretation proved too difficult to understand and coordinate within the group setting. Fortunately, one of the Rohingya group participants spoke both Burmese and Rohingya and was able to translate from Burmese for the other Rohingya participant.

In late December 2016, at the end of the eight-session, arts-focused PTW curriculum, the University of North Carolina (UNC) and ATI facilitators informed the refugee women that the current iteration of the group could only run until late April 2017, when the student facilitators were scheduled to graduate from their master's programs. Following this university-driven timeline, the facilitators asked the women to determine how the remaining four months of the group process should be spent. Within the resulting conversation, one refugee participant spoke firmly about an ongoing issue she was experiencing within the broader community: "When people on the street here talk to me, they think I am deaf. I am not deaf."

Coincidentally, this powerful statement—suggesting persistent language and cultural barriers amid possible antinewcomer sentiment—emerged at the same time that one of the group facilitators from ATI was deciding the focus of her doctoral dissertation research. Although she had originally intended to conduct research with newcomer adolescents within the local school system, a population that had been previously studied at ATI (Kowitt et al., 2016; Rowe et al., 2016), this rallying cry from the Women's Group member suddenly appeared more urgent.

The facilitators decided to ask the women whether they would be open to exploring the aforementioned language and cultural issues through a participatory action research (PAR) project, designed in large part by and for the women. The same refugee participant responded bluntly to this suggestion: "I want to make sure we do something. I want this to be important. I will participate in research if we move *it* to the next level" (italics added). The PAR process detailed next demonstrates how ATI and RW facilitators eventually came to understand the "it" the woman was referring to, and how her goal was ultimately achieved through a new organizational partnership with RCP.

So, What Is PAR?

In its most basic definition, PAR aims to increase the control that participants have over their lives, including the research process (Baum, MacDougall, & Smith, 2006). It seeks to mitigate traditional power differentials between the "researcher" and the "researched" by including participants as equal collaborators in research that addresses issues of their own choosing. PAR expects direct action as a result of the research process and works to reflect "the experience, expertise, and concerns of those who have traditionally been marginalized in the research process and by widely held beliefs about what 'counts' as knowledge" (Brown & Strega, 2005, p. 6).

Participatory research methods thus attempt to offer respectful guidelines of conducting research with and within marginalized and disenfranchised communities. These approaches strive to honor cultural norms as well as elicit holistic and humanized images of research participants. Beyond the current research, anti-oppressive research methods such as PAR have been implemented specifically and successfully within various refugee communities (Borwick, Schweitzer, Brough, Vromans, & Shakespeare-Finch, 2013; Gilhooly & Lynn,

2015; Sonn, Grossman, & Utomo, 2013). Furthermore, several researchers have suggested PAR as the preferred approach to working with refugee women who are often doubly marginalized due to their oppressed gender and nondominant culture (Guruge & Khanlou, 2004; Koh et al., 2013).

Incorporating the Arts

Although this chapter does not focus on the art-based aspect of the research process, it is important to at least note this factor because the embedded artmaking processes both mirrored and deepened the participatory action research process. As described earlier, PAR commits to an iterative practice, shifting with the needs and desires of study participants. Due to this responsive approach, PAR does not typically follow a linear path. Instead, it cycles, weaves in and out, and explores multiple routes to answer the emerging research question(s).

Art-based research (ABR) moves in similar ways. ABR uses artistic expression as a primary mode of enquiry within the research process (Barone & Eisner, 2012; Leavy, 2009; McNiff, 2013). In this type of research, the arts do not typically supplement other primary research methods or act simply as data points. Rather, the arts push the research method forward, serving as the means to create, explore, and analyze information.

The expressive arts also enable flow and attunement (Csikszentmihalyi, 1996; Hinz, 2009; Kossak, 2009). These terms signify that artmaking is an inherently active process, inspiring fluid shifts in thinking and deepening connections and understanding within oneself and between oneself and others. In these ways, artmaking and art-based research resonate with PAR, which also requires action, responds to shifts in thinking, and assumes collaboration, connection, and self-reflection among both researchers and participants. Both PAR and ABR embrace the flexibility needed to meet the messiness and uncertainty that can arise from participatory methods.

Taking It to the Next Level

After in-depth discussions about both PAR and ABR, in January 2017, the refugee women in the health and wellness support group embarked on an art-based participatory action research journey designed to meet their own needs and desires: to "take it to the next level."

The group spent two 2-hour research sessions discussing various potential inquiries related to language and cultural barriers experienced within resettlement and finally settled on the research question: "What are the issues faced by refugee women from Burma living in Orange County, North Carolina, and how can these issues best be communicated and addressed within the greater community?" The women next decided to approach these questions by creating art-based individual and collective narratives focused around the issues they faced. They agreed to share the resulting visual imagery and oral narratives at a dinner party in late April 2017, replete with traditional cultural food they would cook themselves and hosted for the greater community, including local politicians. Finally, the refugee women were interested in putting their narratives online to reach a wider audience.

Although the women appeared to be moving ahead with the research process in these first few sessions, the UNC and ATI facilitators were still becoming anxious that the research would not be completed before the student-facilitators' graduation deadline of April 2017. During the first three research sessions, the refugee women appeared to be circling back on their ideas, essentially starting the process over with every group. Ironically, this circular process completely aligned with PAR ideals. It was the group facilitators who were out of alignment, operating under the confines of a strict schedule that provided little opportunity for the participants to exert agency over the research process or work within their own culturally appropriate timelines.

Importantly, and unsurprisingly, the facilitators' obvious anxiety over completing the research process within the given timeline began to impact the refugee women's anxiety levels as well. The women appeared to believe their group was ending in the spring because not enough refugee women were participating. One woman spoke about how she had tried to recruit new women for the group, but no one she approached was able to attend at the scheduled time. Another woman addressed the facilitators directly: "We know you all are very busy students. We know you don't have time for the Women's Group. It's okay. We understand."

Although the facilitators tried to lessen the women's anxiety by emphasizing how important the group was to them and that termination of the group had nothing to do with the decreased rate of attendance, this task was impossible. The refugee women were correct. Under the prescribed university timeline and mindset, the Women's Group was going to end. The anxiety based on this reality—impacting both facilitators and group members alike—could not be mitigated. Furthermore, the idea that the stability of the Women's Group was out of the refugee women's control was, at its core, disempowering and debilitating. This reality, in itself, went against the ideals of PAR.

Not knowing how to navigate these seemingly contradictory ideas, the group sat in the mess and continued along the PAR process, trusting that if they truly listened to each other, something would emerge and/or resolve. Sure enough, it did.

During the fourth research session, after an exasperated attempt by the UNC and ATI facilitators to narrow down a definitive research plan, a dramatic shift in power and purpose occurred. Instead of directing their research action steps outward (toward U.S. community members, politicians, and blogpost readers, as they had originally desired), the refugee women suddenly adamantly refocused their research efforts internally—within their own community. They no longer wanted to share their ideas with "others" outside of their cultural community but were committed, instead, to serving "other women from Burma." One refugee group member painted "I love Women's Group" in bold, black lettering across four pieces of colored fabric and verbally explained, "I want the Women's Group to be strong and stable." The other women in the group quickly echoed this sentiment.

Strength and Stability

When the women began consistently asking, "How can we make this group strong and stable?", it became obvious that the impact of the research—and possibly the research process itself—needed to extend beyond the academic timeline. It also now seemed deeply inadequate for the research to focus on a singular, product-driven project, such as a dinner party or blog post. The new research question inspired and required continuity, trust, and deep, ongoing relationships. It also required the group facilitators to recommit to the PAR process—to reflect critically on their research practices and listen fully to the women's needs and desires.

On an even larger scale, the new research question—"How can we make this group strong and stable?"—seemed to mirror the instability of the broader world in which the women found themselves living. Notably, the shift in the research inquiry occurred two weeks after the new Trump administration issued an executive order banning refugees from Muslim-majority countries from entering the United States. This ban seemed to exacerbate a sense of instability among the women, who were suddenly deeply uncertain about the status of refugees in the United States as well as the status of their small, yet vital Women's Group.

Hence, beginning in March 2017, the research group committed to exploring the newly defined topic of strength and stability through collective, expressive arts directives. The anxiety of both the group facilitators and refugee women began to subside as the research process realigned with the needs and desires of the women and as the ideals of PAR were rediscovered. ATI and RW facilitators now worked side by side with the women, utilizing art-based processes to identify and share personal strengths, strengths of the group, and possible approaches to achieving future stability of the Women's Group. Instead of talking at the refugee women, the facilitators talked with them. More important, the facilitators learned to listen.

A New Collaboration Emerges

In the beginning of March 2017, the director of the Refugee Wellness program, a professor at UNC–Chapel Hill—understanding the needs of the refugee women but also recognizing the university's inability to continue coleading the Women's Group due to the student-facilitators' impending graduation date and the larger uncertainty of future RW programmatic funding—connected Hillary to Madison. Through this meeting, Hillary discovered that the RCP had just started leading its own Women's Group for refugees from Burma, and there was already overlap between group participants. Together, Hillary and Maddie approached the idea of what a collaborative group would look like, and Hillary agreed to bring this idea to the research participants.

During the sixth research group, Hillary shared that she and Maddie were considering the feasibility of a collaborative, community-based Women's Group that was not beholden to the university's demands. The women's faces brightened at the possibility. One of the participants held Hillary's hand throughout the entire discussion, repeatedly asking, "So the Women's Group will not end?" She smiled with her teeth for the first time.

The following cannot be understated: In direct response to the PAR driven by the refugee women from Burma, the Women's Group continues to this day. ATI not only teamed up with RCP to strengthen and stabilize the Women's Group for perpetuity, they also chose to co-rent a new office space with RCP to further ease and solidify future project collaborations and funding partnerships. In summary, the refugee women's research project inspired concrete organizational change.

Was this the goal of the refugee women? Most likely, not. Their goal was to strengthen and stabilize their beloved Women's Group by any means necessary. Still, it must be noted that, by truly listening to the women's priorities, local community organizations recognized the need to expand services and worked alongside the women to achieve this goal through collaboration and resource sharing.

Today, both ATI and RCP staff and volunteers co-lead the women's group. Every month, the refugee women are asked to determine a topic they want to address the following session, and a combination of verbal conversations, expressive therapies directives, and presentations by outside community organizations are then implemented to help achieve the women's stated goals. RCP volunteers help transport the women to the group as needed and provide child care in an adjacent room during the session. ATI works to secure grants to purchase art supplies and pay for clinical therapists and professional interpreters as needed. Many times, however, the refugee women interpret for and counsel one another.

The mission of the new collaborative group, written by the refugee women, is

To empower, support, educate and protect one another as women who have arrived in the area with refugee status; to educate one another regarding the many challenges that we encounter in a new place and culture; and to connect one another to resources that assist in helping address problems we have.

This mission seems to reflect the women's original research question: "What are the issues faced by refugee women from Burma living in Orange County, North Carolina, and how can these issues best be communicated and addressed within the greater community?" These questions could not be approached on a broader scale until more basic and immediate needs—such as stabilizing the Women's Group—had been met.

Looking back on the research study now, it is clear that this process reflected trauma-informed care, which asserts that safety and stability must be established before deeper issues can be addressed (Rosenbalm, 2017). Although the refugee women might not have recognized or labeled their actions as trauma-informed, their thoughtful and thorough processes showed that they knew exactly what they needed and knew exactly what they were doing. Again, all the facilitators had to do was listen.

Disrupting the Western Research Paradigm

The case study detailed one successful example of how community-driven research questions can be identified and answered. It is equally important to ask and answer questions about the practice of research. In a transparent effort to do just this, we end our chapter by reflecting critically on what this particular research process and our new organizational collaboration have taught us.

There is something deeply humbling about participatory action research. For us academics, it presents opportunities to reflect on the research process as well as the historical arc of research, its complicated relationship with researched communities, and other existential considerations. Why conduct research? Who should be in charge of determining research question(s)? Where and when should research be conducted? How should data be collected, analyzed, and disseminated? What does the research process feel like to everyone involved? What will the impact of the research be, and who will be impacted?

It is the work of the researcher to ask herself these types of questions—to wrestle with the long colonial history of academic research sciences that have constituted disenfranchised communities more as objects of research rather than authorities about their own ways of knowing, doing, and being. Whose are the voices of authority? Who makes the decisions? Who is diagnosing the problem? The decolonization of research methodologies is a long-term process of handing over the microscope as well as the divestment from the parameters of the dominant paradigm (Staehelin, 2000). As researchers, we have the choice to perpetuate or interrupt this paradigm.

The premise that Western research is for the greater good is one that captured and inspired most of us to enter the industry. Without a critical analysis of the ways in which the Western tradition of knowledge positions Western constructs, codifications, and norms by smothering out those of non-Anglo European descent, the premise will be held in vain.

"Legitimate" Knowledge

Scholars have long articulated critiques of the colonization of social inquiry, which has produced what some refer to as the "era of the expert," where "legitimate" knowledge is sanctioned by the academy. It confers authority to us professionals. This has produced significant blind spots in our understanding of people, and it invalidates their wisdom and robs them of their own agency.

What can be most detrimental to our research is that, without the expertise and wisdom of participant communities from the start, we often wind up diagnosing the wrong problem or asking the wrong questions. The argument for PAR methodologies posits PAR as a resolution to the often conflicting goals between the university and the community, the hierarchical relation of power that privileges academic knowledge over community wisdom, and community-identified problems and needs (Zavala, 2013).

Beyond Cultural Competence

Researchers and practitioners often strive for cultural competence in their work, but "competence" implies that a satisfactory endpoint has been achieved. Cultural humility, in contrast, asserts that it is impossible to be adequately knowledgeable about any culture other than one's own (Levi, 2009). Cultural humility involves a decentering of the self through constant questioning, self-reflection, and commitment to learning about others. It requires that we consistently assess our own limitations, the gaps in our knowledge, and our ability and willingness to disrupt our understanding of the world and our position in it.

Committing to cultural humility is a critical and deliberate research practice. When practitioners interview clients, the client is the expert on her own life, symptoms, and strengths. The client holds a body of knowledge that the practitioner does not (Waters & Asbill, 2013). This body of knowledge will determine how a question is answered as well as what questions are relevant and which aren't. This reality contends that communities should be involved in the "problem-diagnosing" process, where their expertise and wisdom inform the question asking and decision making from the start. Without their expertise, researchers will ask the wrong questions.

When those in traditional roles of power are the ones setting the environment—from aesthetics, to language and terminology, to social norms, standards, and expectations—we discourage participation, at best; at worst, we perpetuate the isolation and social division that participants experience in their daily lives. Cultivating a culturally safe environment requires first naming and then addressing the personal and structural power dynamics at play (Reavy, Hobbs, Hereford, & Crawford, 2012).

Anti-oppressive research (AOR) exposes the problematic power dynamics found in traditional research practices by moving beyond stating values of diversity and inclusion. AOR critically examines the concept of safety, specifically considering who determines what safety looks like. Just because researchers label an environment as safe does not ensure safety for research participants. Research is only safe if participants feel safe, and this requires that participants determine how, where, and when research is conducted.

Without participants in control of the research pathway, culturally violent spaces will continue to be replicated by researchers.

Imagine a carpeted conference room with vaulted ceilings and fluorescent lighting on a university campus buzzing with young, White, English-speaking students. Now, imagine a verdant farm, with thatched-roof huts and a bamboo platform for sitting, studded with bowls of rice and grasses for fanning. Between a White researcher and a participant from, say, Burma, it is clear who constructed which. Can we suspect in which space the participant will feel more comfortable, more "herself," more physically, psychologically, and culturally "safe," more disposed to own the "expert" role? In which space is her cultural identity affirmed and validated, and in which is it invalidated? These are the questions we should be asking ourselves, because the answers will radically change the research process and the data that it produces.

Smiling with Our Teeth

The office space that ATI and RCP now share is situated in the middle of the host community along a free bus route. The refugee women are encouraged to bring in traditional cultural food to share with others during group sessions, if they desire. Their children run freely through the large lobby area adjacent to the group room, squealing and creating art with community volunteers. Babies sleep peacefully in strollers around the group room, and when they stir, they are passed from woman to woman to be cradled. The refugee women sit in a circle alongside RCP and ATI staff and volunteers, as we share our individual and collective stories through art and words.

We build trust with one another and, step by step, with our neighbors from other cultures, as we invite them into our group space to speak about local resources and discuss the complexities of the community we share. We advocate for our needs, empowering one another to identify and answer our own questions. We try, in whatever ways we can, to create a sense of strength and stability in an unstable and unjust world. We squeeze each other's hands in solidarity and support. We smile with our teeth.

References

American Art Therapy Association. (2017). *About art therapy*. Retrieved from https://arttherapy.org/about-art-therapy/

Appel, M. (2012). Anti-immigrant propaganda by radical right parties and the intellectual performance of adolescents. *Political Psychology, 33*(4), 483–493.

Baird, M. B., Domian, E. W., Mulcahy, E. R., Mabior, R., Jemutai-Tanui, G., & Filippi, M. K. (2015). Creating a bridge of understanding between two worlds: Community-based collaborative-action research with Sudanese refugee women. *Public Health Nursing, 32*(5), 388-396.

Barone, T., & Eisner, E. (2012). *Arts-based research*. Thousand Oaks, CA: Sage.

Barron, S., Okell, J., Yin, S. W., Vanbik, K., Swain, A., Larkin, E. . . . Ewers, K. (2007). *Refugees from Burma: Their backgrounds and refugee experiences*. Washington DC: Cultural Orientation Resource Center, Center for Applied Linguistics. Retrieved from file:///Users/WTF/Downloads/refugeesfromburma%20(2).pdf

Baum, F., MacDougall, C., & Smith, D. (2006). Participatory action research. *Journal of Epidemiology and Community Health, 60*(10), 854-857.

Borwick, S., Schweitzer, R. D., Brough, M., Vromans, L., & Shakespeare-Finch, J. (2013). Well-being of refugees from Burma: A salutogenic perspective. *International Migration, 51*(5), 91-105.

Brown, L., & Strega, S. (Eds.). (2005). *Research as resistance: Critical, indigenous, and anti-oppressive approaches*. Toronto, Ontario: Canadian Scholars' Press/Women's Press.

Cathcart, R., Decker, C., Ellenson, M., & Amell, J. (2007). *People from Burma living in Chapel Hill and Carrboro: An action-oriented community diagnosis: Findings and next steps of action*. Unpublished paper. University of North Carolina at Chapel Hill, Chapel Hill, NC.

Chantler, K. (2012). Gender, asylum seekers and mental distress: Challenges for mental health social work. *British Journal of Social Work, 42*, 318–334.

Clark, A., Gilbert, A., Rao, D., & Kerr, L. (2014). "Excuse me, do any of you ladies speak English?" Perspectives of refugee women living in South Australia: Barriers to accessing primary health care and achieving the quality use of medicines. *Australian Journal of Primary Health, 20*(1), 92–97.

Clifford, S. (2016). Refugee arrival trends [Meeting handout]. Orange County Health Department, Chapel Hill, NC.

Collie, P., Liu, J., Podsiadlowski, A., & Kindon, S. (2010). You can't clap with one hand: Learnings to promote culturally grounded participatory action research with migrant and former refugee communities. *International Journal of Intercultural Relations, 34*, 141-149.

Connor, J. J., Hunt, S., Finsaas, M., Ciesinski, A., Ahmed, A., & Robinson, B. "Bean" E. (2016). From Somalia to U.S.: Shifts in gender dynamics from the perspective of female Somali refugees. *Journal of Feminist Family Therapy, 28*(1), 1–29.

Crosby, S. S. (2013). Primary care management of non–English-speaking refugees who have experienced trauma. *JAMA, 310*(5), 519-528.

Csikszentmihalyi, M. (1996). *Creativity: Flow and the psychology of discovery and invention.* New York, NY: Harper Perennial.

Dieterich-Hartwell, R., & Koch, S. (2017). Creative arts therapies as temporary home for refugees: Insights from literature and practice. *Behavioral Sciences, 7*(4), 69.

Ellenson, M. D. (2008). *Migration to health through art: A grant proposal for art therapy for refugee children from Burma in the Chapel Hill/Carrboro City Schools.* Unpublished doctoral dissertation. University of North Carolina at Chapel Hill, Chapel Hill, NC.

Ellis, B. H., MacDonald, H. Z., Lincoln, A. K., & Cabral, H. J. (2008). Mental health of Somali adolescent refugees: The role of trauma, stress, and perceived discrimination. *International Journal of Emergency Mental Health, 10*(2), 161-162.

Gilhooly, D., & Lynn, C. A. (2015). Karen resettlement: A participatory action research project. *International Migration & Integration, 16,* 799-817.

Guruge, S., & Khanlou, N. (2004). Intersectionalities of influence: Researching the health of immigrant and refugee women. *Canadian Journal of Nursing Research, 36*(3), 32-47.

Hinz, L. D. (2009). *Expressive therapies continuum.* New York, NY: Taylor & Francis.

Koh, L. C., Liamputtong, P., & Walker, R. (2013). Burmese refugee young women navigating parental expectations and resettlement. *Journal of Family Studies, 19*(3), 297-305.

Kossak, M. S. (2009). Therapeutic attunement: A transpersonal view of expressive arts therapy. *Arts in Psychotherapy, 36*(1), 13–18.

Kowitt, S. D., Emmerling, D., Gavarkavich, D., Mershon, C.-H., Linton, K., Rubesin, H., . . . Eng, E. (2016). A pilot evaluation of an art therapy program for refugee youth from Burma. *Art Therapy, 33*(1), 13-20.

Leavy, P. (2009). *Methods meet art.* New York, NY: Guilford.

Levi, A. (2009). The ethics of nursing student international clinical experiences. *Journal of Obstetric, Gynecologic, and Neonatal Nursing, 38*(1), 94-99.

McNiff, S. (Ed.). (2013). *Art as research: Opportunities and challenges.* Chicago, IL: Intellect, Ltd.

Millington, G. (2010). Racism, class ethos and place: The value of context in narratives about asylum-seekers. *Sociological Review, 58*(3), 361–380.

Morris, M. D., Popper, S. T., Rodwell, T. C., Brodine, S. K., & Brouwer, K. C. (2009). Healthcare barriers of refugees post-resettlement. *Journal of Community Health, 34*(6), 529–538.

Newman, B. J., Hartman, T. K., & Taber, C. S. (2012). Foreign language exposure, cultural threat, and opposition to immigration. *Political Psychology, 33*(5), 635–657.

Norsworthy, K. L., & Khuankaew, O. (2004). Women of Burma speak out: Workshops to deconstruct gender-based violence and build systems of peace and justice. *The Journal for Specialists in Group Work, 29*(3), 259-283.

Okigbo, C., Reierson, J., & Stowman, S. (2009). Leveraging acculturation through action research. *Action Research, 7*(2), 127-142.

Pathways to Wellness. (2011). *Pathways to Wellness: Integrating refugee health and well-being: Creating pathways for refugee survivors to heal.* Retrieved from https://cls.unc.edu/files/2015/06/RHS15_Packet_PathwaysToWellness.pdf

Pedersen, A., & Thomas, E. (2013). "There but for the grace of God go we": Prejudice toward asylum seekers. *Peace and Conflict: Journal of Peace Psychology, 19*(3), 253-265.

Pew Research Center (2017). *Where have refugees settled in the US?* Retrieved from http://www.pewglobal.org/interactives/where-have-refugees-settled-in-the-u-s/

Radford, J., & Connor, P. (2016). Just 10 states resettled half of recent refugees to U.S. *Pew Research Center.* Retrieved from http://www.pewresearch.org/fact-tank/2016/12/06/just-10-states-resettled-more-than-half-of-recent-refugees-to-u-s/

Reavy, K., Hobbs, J., Hereford, M., & Crawford, K. (2012). A new clinic model for refugee health care: Adaptation of cultural safety. *Rural and Remote Health, 12* (1826), 1-12.

Rosenbalm, K. (2017). "Trauma-informed strategies for educators." NC Resilience & Learning Project. *Duke Center for Child and Family Policy* (PowerPoint Presentation).

Rowe, C., Watson-Ormond, R., English, L., Rubesin, H., Marshall, A., Linton, K., . . . Eng, E. (2016). Evaluating art therapy to heal the effects of trauma among refugee youth. *Health Promotion Practice, 18*(1), 26–33.

Schweitzer, R. D., Brough, M., Vromans, L., & Asic-Kobe, M. (2011). Mental health of newly arrived Burmese refugees in Australia: Contributions of pre-migration and post-migration experience. *Australian and New Zealand Journal of Psychiatry, 45,* 299-307.

Sonn, C. C., Grossman, M., & Utomo, A. (2013). Reflections on a participatory research project: Young people of refugee background in an arts-based program. *Journal for Social Action in Counseling and Psychology, 5*(3), 95-110.

Staehelin, I. M. (March, 2000). Decolonizing methodologies: Research and indigenous peoples. *Cultural Survival.* Retrieved from https://www.culturalsurvival.org/publications/cultural-survival-quarterly/decolonizing-methodologies-research-and-indigenous-peoples

U.S. Census Bureau. (2015). *North Carolina becomes ninth state with 10 million or more people, Census Bureau reports.* Retrieved from https://www.census.gov/newsroom/press-releases/2015/cb15-215.html

U.S. Census Bureau. (2017). *Quick facts, Orange County, North Carolina.* Retrieved from https://www.census.gov/quickfacts/fact/map/orangecountynorthcarolina/PST045217

United Nations High Commissioner for Refugees. (2016). *Global forced displacement hits record high.* Retrieved from http://www.unhcr.org/en-us/news/latest/2016/6/5763b65a4/global-forced-displacement-hits-record-high.html

Waters, A., & Asbill, L. (2013). Reflections on cultural humility. *American Psychological Association*. Retrieved from http://www.apa.org/pi/families/resources/newsletter/2013/08/cultural-humility.aspx

Watkins, P. G., Razee, H., & Richters, J. (2012). "I'm telling you... the language barrier is the most, the biggest challenge": Barriers to education among Karen refugee women in Australia. *Australian Journal of Education, 56*(2), 126–141. Retrieved from http://ezproxy.scu.edu.au/login?url=http://search.ebscohost.com/login.aspx?direct=true&db=eric&AN=EJ980305&site=ehost-live%5Cnhttp://www.acer.edu.au/press/aje/contents1

Zavala, M. (2013). What do we mean by decolonizing research strategies? Lessons from decolonizing, Indigenous research projects in New Zealand and Latin America. *Decolonization: Indigeneity, Education & Society, 2*(1), 55-71.

CHAPTER 6

Cyborg Scholarship
Films for the People

M. Francyne Huckaby

THIS CHAPTER, BASED on the digitally born ethnographic film project, *Public Education: Participatory Democracy After Neoliberal Times*, is feminist scholarship born of necessity. It witnesses, documents, analyzes, and (re)presents the counterstories and activism of marginalized and displaced communities in the struggle to claim education at a time when receiving it is threatened. My camera and I, together, become the living camera, the participatory camera, the cine-eye-ear—cyborg—exploring cyborg weaving as a renewed possibility for participatory democracy.

Introduction

If you were expecting a cyborg, something like a kinky-haired, full-hipped Borg Queen (Bergman & Frakes, 1996), I'm sorry to disappoint. Nonetheless, here we are: human and machine. We are here to share our story, travels, and methodology about how we became cyborg and came to filmmaking. Although I was already cyborg when I first began relying on machines to become, express, and know myself, I was unaware of this hybrid existence until I turned to filmmaking out of necessity in early 2013. My camera and I became the participatory camera (Luc de Heusch; cited in Rouch, 1973), the cine-eye-ear (Rouch, 1973): cyborg (Image 6.1).

My eye attunes to the digital lens; my ear surveys the soundscape. Less concerned with what I see and hear, my senses assimilate to technology that records and re-creates light, moving images and sound. With a tiny machine integrating into my being; we become the living, participatory camera, the cine-eye-ear, cyborg woman/machine. (Huckaby, 2017, p. 340)

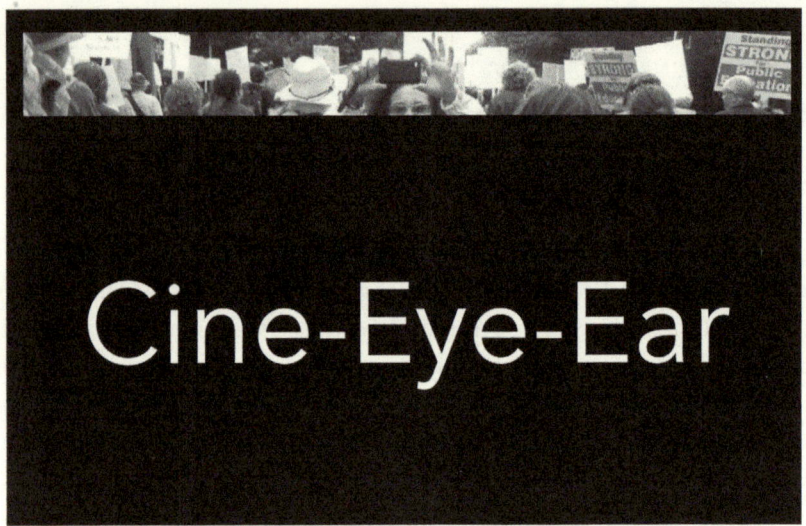

Image 6.1. *Cine-eye-ear visual from the presentation*

That I, a luddite, am cyborg is ironic. A daughter of IBM employees, I resisted computers, likely as a form of adolescent rebellion. A portable all-in-one computer appeared on the desk in the kitchen one day. This was a historic event, yet it captured none of my attention. In college I gave in to computers because they aided my procrastination. Instead of thinking, writing, and then typing, I found I could think, write, and type in one action; this was revolutionary. I was as reluctant with cell phones, smart phones, and tablets. I thought a laptop computer and 500 GB was all I needed for the 21st century. When tablets came out, I also ignored them, believing they would just be redundancies of the services my laptop offered. However, their portability and versatility, particularly the audiovisual recording features, caught my scholarly eye. Instead of carrying around paper consent forms, recorders, batteries, camera, and so on, I could pack one flat device, a charging cord, and an adapter. So this compact digital device started out as my film equipment during sabbatical. I had no way of knowing that I would build up to a 40 TB data storage capacity that automatically duplicates each saved file. We, my machines and I, currently hold 14 terabytes or 14,336 gigabytes, and we are contemplating the next capacity upgrade.

Joining the Struggle

In 2013, I had just finished my sabbatical in Chicago and New York, where I immersed myself in the grassroots struggle to maintain, sustain, and improve neighborhood public schools. I sought to understand and explore the perspectives and to witness participatory democracy of those who ended up on the losing end of the No Child Left Behind Act (NCLB) and Race to the Top (RTTT). I also sought to study the impact of and community critical engagement with privatization and neoliberalism as education reform. By critical engagement, I refer to how organized groups actively enter with conscious intent to transform relations of power around schooling. By privatization I mean the impositions of competition, choice, accountability, and marketing into schooling as well as the opening of school funding to private entities and transferring public resources (including money) to private entities. Neoliberalism then is a shaping of an individualism that ignores the ways in which systemic and systematic processes privilege and disadvantage. It is a discourse that relegates the social to the isolated consumer (Giroux, 2008) that was formed over decades and centuries of discourses, practices, transformations, and disruptions that form us into *homoeconomicous* (Foucault, 2008). If you are under 50 years old, this is the world known to you, much like a fish knows water without knowing "the weight of the water" (Bourdieu & Wacquant, 1992, p. 127). For those over 50 years old, memories of other ways of being in society flicker in and out of consciousness as if you were fish out of water.

Prior to 2012, I had no intention of studying community responses to education laws and policy. I was into theory, philosophy, critical qualitative research, and aesthetic forms of inquiry. I had found my way into a scholarly life concerned with social justice and equity. While I had not avoided conducting studies connected to the impact of policy and law, I did not do such research myself. I felt others were better educated and suited for such work—those in policy studies, political science, history, psychometrics, and so forth. During my early academic career, modeling for NCLB projected the proposed law would result in about half of public schools failing by 2012 or 2014. These models showed the way the system would work, sans specifics of life in individual schools or abilities of actual students. They revealed the ways NCLB set schools up for competition that was not dissimilar to sport competitions, where those with higher scores progress with rewards and those with lower scores would be identified annually and suffer designated penalties. I imagine the architects of NCLB thought schools and communities might play along by displaying good sportsmanship. However, unlike sports games where eliminated teams can come back the next year to play, closed schools were/are completely excluded. I thought this law was ridiculous, that struggling schools needed additional resources and supports, that the standardized test scores of students and their schools should take into consideration the resources put into schools as well as the language and cognitive abilities of students vis-á-vis the language and level of the tests. "Surely," I thought, "people sharper on the topic than I would, could reveal to politicians and policy makers the errs they faced." Some did try, but the predictions held.

In 2005, a surge of water formed by Hurricane Katrina broke the levies in New Orleans, making much of the city unlivable for a time, creating a rationalization for the recovery school district, and hastening the transition that transformed nearly all public schools into charter schools. These changes in New Orleans, executed in a hastened fashion, tested the trajectory of NCLB and foreshadowed changes to come in other urban areas with Brown, Black, and poor students. RTTT came along in 2009, giving NCLB a steroidal boost (Ravitch, 2013). Closer to home, Texas cut its education budget by $5.3 billion in 2011 (Castro, 2011; del Conte & Hornberger, 2014), a time when schools needed additional resources. The absurdity of these actions and the impact they had on communities, especially Black, Brown, poor, and immigrant communities, compelled me as an educator and citizen to bring them into my scholarship. Thus, my Chicago and New York sabbatical during the 2012 fall semester was research born of necessity more so than my research interests and agenda. Because I wanted to heed Margaret Mead's advice about relying on "pencil and notebook" when film had so much to offer (Crawford & Turton, 1992, p. 3), I brought along my tablet so that I could audiorecord interviews as well as photograph and film events. I expected to use this device much like I would have a notebook and pen: to record digital field notes that would lead to writing. My goal was to write a book, my first one. A book of scholarly origin, but written for a lay audience, would potentially reach more people than articles published in academic journals. I imagined that images from my digital record would be a nice addition to such a book. And then my sabbatical ended. I began writing.

My scholarship has always been about the struggle, for use in the struggle, so I thought I knew what to expect. Had I not been in cities with active, organized movements to intervene and make public the ways the school boards and districts treated students, their families, teachers, school personnel, and schools, I would have been overwhelmed and likely paralyzed into inaction, at least for a while. But becoming part of the movement, as a participant and researcher, offered an effective antidote. I did not anticipate the pushback I would get for this project. I saw it as no more political than my other work, which is a more explicitly theoretical and philosophical exploration of relations of asymmetrical power and vulnerability. But this turn in my work brought resistance. The first form of resistance I faced was funding the project. Most of the grants I identified sought research proposals that would foster knowledge friendly to school choice and competition. I believe that because my work was running counter to the more accepted political rhetoric of school choice and competition, it was deemed too political by some and not the funding priority for others. Scholarship that focuses on school choice and competition is not neutral. The knowledge that created such conceptions and the processes that make it seem natural were/are political. The new knowledges that researchers produce make changes in the world and in people's lives. Even though I am not a disinterested scholar, my scholarship is no more political than work that pushes neoliberalism forward. Furthermore, I propose that no researcher is neutral. However, because my research questions law, policy, and established rhetoric; because I focus more on poor communities and communities of color; and because I offer stories that counter hegemony, my research is deemed political and other work neutral. Many may assume, for example, that medical research in pursuit of a cure is apolitical. Doing research to make a change in the world, to reduce the suffering of people, is political in that the action to find a cure for one disease and not another may reduce suffering for some but not others. That researchers might choose to study diseases due to personal interests (e.g., loved ones who had the disease or concerns about how the disease might harm a particular group or transform a society) points to the ways the personal is political and vice versa. Focusing research funding, resources, and efforts on prostate cancer more so than ovarian cancer is political and affects men and women differently. In late 2011 and early 2012, I found myself in a world with most foundation support for public education targeted toward research and initiatives of the neoliberal ilk. Such venture philanthropy merges corporate philanthropy with venture capitalism to shape education reform nationally and influence it in local cities with the desires of billionaires (Kumashiro, 2012; Lipman & Jenkins, 2011; Watkins, 2004). Even when I found funding sources that supported equitable and just public education on the surface with their language, closer inspection often showed otherwise. All work to improve life requires choices to attend to something and ignore some other things. In the case of education reform, the better world promised by competition and choice has also meant educational disenfranchisement and destabilization of minoritized communities. Atwood (1986) expressed this idea in *The Handmaid's Tale*: "Better never means better for everyone ... It always means worse, for some" (p. 211).

Writing the Struggle

My intent is that this project offers possibilities that St. Pierre and Pillow (2000) propose: "possibilities for different worlds that might, perhaps, not be so cruel to so many people ... that produce different knowledge and produce knowledge differently, thereby producing different ways of living in the world" (p. 1). Drawing on Foucault's (1997) notion of games of truth, I wanted to address this question: How do those who lose show the consequences of the game and work to make another reality? I knew that in the process of addressing this question, I would have to share context that provided answers to the questions posed by Guinier and Torres (2003) and reiterated by Kumashiro (2012) and Lewis:[1] Who are the winners and the losers? Who makes the rules? What do the winners tell the losers so that they keep playing? As I wrote, I shared text within informal contexts and conferences in my local area, nationally, and internationally. I wanted to see how audiences would respond to this scholarship, which focused on the activity of speaking up, of activism, of organized movement building as I continued writing. Members of audiences who had experienced the negative impact of corporate education reform appreciated the work and focus on what people were doing in organized efforts. The work gave them an opportunity to know their struggle was not just theirs and to compare their activism with others. Audience members who wanted corporate education reform were interested in my work about organizing around high-stakes testing, but they vehemently challenged that related to community activism in response to charter schools, school turnaround programs, school closings, and so forth. I believe they found it difficult to conceive of school districts actually disenfranchising students in a post-*Brown* world; that the *Brown v. Board of Education* (1954) decision had solved the real school inequities, and that choice and competition were the next step. That such policies would further exacerbate inequalities they thought no longer existed was a perturbation, I believed. They thought school choice, competition, and the closing of failing schools were good reforms for U.S. education, and they responded to my scholarship as though it were too political.

So, I started again with the task of describing what was happening in public education—to students, families, school personnel, and communities—that fostered the need for community organizing and activism in cities like Chicago and New York. By extending my study to Houston,[2] I offered a local example to counter dismissal of my work in the South because it studied northern cities. I explained high-stakes testing, turnaround programs, the impact that corporate charter schools and vouchers have on neighborhood public schools, school closings, and the shuffling of youth from closed schools to other schools vulnerable for closure. The world had again marked Black and Brown students with limited monetary resources and political influence. Students in the segregated schools were deemed disposable by policymakers and budget managers to make room for new schools and reconstituted schools that did not serve them. I didn't want to reify this system; I wanted to amplify how people organized movements to create a different reality, to make real the kinds of schools they deserve (Image 6.2).

Image 6.2. *One sign from a series naming what Chicago public school students deserve*

In response to audiences of my readings, I began explicating the school reform that deformed (Pinar, 2004). I found myself moving further away from my intended question with revisions that would better prepare audiences to more seriously consider the study of activism I wanted to explore and more toward those about winners, losers, rules of the games, and enticements to play. These questions placed more attention on the winners and rule makers while hiding the impact of the structures they built. This meant that my work pointed to simulacra (Baudrillard, 1983; Bogard, 1987; Lather, 1993)—models of a real without origin in reality. Test scores are real measurements, but they are not learning. School rankings and ratings are things for publishing and marketing, but they are not environments supportive of learning. Growth models are data for deciding, but they are not the fulfillment of human potential or the journey of youth in their becoming. Simulacra are truths that reveal and conceal that there is none. Interestingly, no one questioned me over testing. I was not sure whether they thought I imposed macabre fantasies or was too sympathetic with people who are Black, Brown, immigrant, or poor.

Rewriting the Struggle as Cyborg

I, however, wanted to notice the people who were losing, refused to continue to lose, and chose to play a different game differently (Foucault, 1997)—those who exposed the structures and processes working against them and collectively sought out ways to circumvent, interrupt, redirect, and create anew. Elsewhere in an *International Review of Qualitative Research* (*IRQR*) special issue on critical qualitative inquiry that would expand "theoretically informed, engaged activism" (Koro-Ljungberg & Cannella, 2017, p. 327), I have written about how this conundrum led to my pursuit of film as inquiry that extends my scholarship and transformed me into cyborg (Huckaby, 2017). My work is not that unlike Edward Muybridge, who wanted to know and share how a horse trotted with film, technically a cinematograph, to an audience that assumed horses' legs reach out forward and behind instead of in and under when all four hooves are off the ground (Rouch, 1973). The cinematograph revealed motion that countered conventional wisdom and artistic renderings of the time. Similarly, film has offered me a means to share what people experience and to do so in shorts that range from 30 seconds to three or even 17 minutes. The shorts express much in terms of layered meaning and create time for me to address my intended question of what people struggle for and how they do it; a space where viewer-reader-audiences do not remain preoccupied with winners, losers, and rules. Unlike Muybridge, however, I did not have to invent a new method and technologies. Instead, I turned to technology in existence—technology that transformed me from a writing scholar into a cyborg (Huckaby, 2017).

At first I began integrating still images into my papers and grant proposals (much like I have here) and film clips into my presentations. As I developed my skills through practice, trial and error, and a couple of film classes at my university, I began making short films. I awaited feedback and watched responses, which I used to revise shorts and create additional films. I used every conference paper and invited address I could to push the project further, to develop another short, to test whether a shorter or longer version better engaged the audience, to create a short for a different audience, to make a longer cut. We, my machines and their human, continued to follow the movement, to be part of the movement, and to expand the stories we tell in our films.

Because film has the capacity to disrupt past assumptions, it encourages critical thinking through the senses (Wood, 2015). This project invites viewer-readers into the counterstories and activism of marginalized and displaced communities as they struggle to claim their education (Rich, 1995) at a time when receiving it is threatened. This is feminist research born of necessity. I put feminist and Black feminist theory to use in the intellectual shaping of this project and its methodology. I study at the intersection of the private/public, reproductive/productive, home/society. Grumet (1988), Rich (1995), Martin (1981), and Arendt (1961) help us understand the separation made in gendering and feminizing the private realm, the home, and those reproductive processes of society that renew and transition. Schooling is such a space that transforms minor children into adults politically formed for their society, transferring them from the protected home to a productive society, delivering them from the mother to the patriarchy. The diasporas of feminist movements that have spread across this planet are teaching us that the personal is political as it reveals the ways the public, productive forces constrain through feminization. "To be feminized means to be made extremely vulnerable; able to be disassembled, reassembled, exploited as a reserve labor force; seen less as workers than as servers; . . ." (Haraway, 1991, loc. 3402). Education is a feminized profession, and as Pinar (2004) has noted, "desegregation coded public education as 'feminized' and 'black'" (p. xii).

This project of counternarratives resists the constraints of feminization. Most films about education turn to people who can present a convincing narrative—mostly male, White, authoritative—to theorize about what to do, who to do it to, and why. This project is about people in the struggle. I listen to them as they speak and theorize without need of authorities doing either for them. I am a participant of the struggle, and I struggle to create work that does not further marginalize and can be useful as we co-create a just world. As a critical qualitative researcher, however, I must remain vigilant to representation and how viewers/readers respond. To do so I attend to how they make sense of what I share through the senses stimulated by film.

To foster critical thinking through the senses, I ensure that my films are diverse in race, gender, socioeconomic status, and roles. I want viewer-readers to see people speaking about their experiences, explicating their own theorizing, and determining their solutions. I suspect they will feel the absence of the expected authorities, who are too often male, White, and more financially secure, but I have no desire to reify the myths of the hero, savior, or wise wo/man as they interrupt and halt the communal work of knowledge-making and social justice. Instead, I present moving image-light-sound of poli-image-vocal film-text that challenges the implicit biases about who can speak, theorize, and problem solve as well as assumptions that corporate education reform is good for everyone and that all parents and students want school choice and competition. I offer ways to restructure political action theoretically and practically with film that makes present peoples and communities that are too often absent. I choose to focus on local people in the struggle and not its celebrities. Early in the project, this choice was hard to make. I know that if my project featured famous people, it would likely garner more attention. I avoided this route. Nevertheless, I have to admit that some of the people I filmed are gaining in their public recognition.

I make the absence of community sensed when images focus on individuals as talking heads by translating theory into moving image-light-sound. In an *IRQR* article (Huckaby, 2017), I explicated my concept of symbolic illumination and explained the importance of symbolic space in my films. I use voids and black space around the close-ups and wide shots for groups in action (Image 6.3), making the shared work occupy more visual symbolic space (Bourdieu, Sapiro, & McHale, 1991) than the individual. Viewers notice the absence of the group in the partially empty screen of the individual, and I hope they anticipate a reconnection to collective action or imagine themselves as part of those absent with each individual close-up. Symbolic illumination alters the light and demands that the eye adjust by dilating the iris with the close-ups and black background and constricting with the full screen of group action whether viewed with projector, TV, computer, or handheld device. These changes in symbolic illumination (Huckaby, 2017) and symbolic space provide a differential symbolism between the individual and the collective, between the expected documentary trope of authority and the poli-image-vocality of my films, between darker and lighter projects, and between image-filled and partially void screens. This I intend to be a corrective action to the individualization and consumerization of the individual so essential to neoliberalism.

Cyborg Weaving and the Struggle

Film as scholarship requires the filmmaker to remain a scholar. This means that, at times, my films violate expectations of cinematic audiences. For example, I stopped asking people to repeat themselves for cinematic appeal. The second take was always more rehearsed and constructed better, but it had less feeling and intentionality. This means I leave some fumbling over words, extraneous environmental sounds, and unexpected visual presences in my films. I worry more about the images and sounds recorded in the field than creating soundtracks and graphics to accompany my films. In terms of cinematic appeal, the limited use of music slows down the films, which is risky because audiences are used to a fast pace. But sound vibrates through our bodies in such complicated ways and adds layers of emotion that a viewer may not experience without the added soundtrack. The absence of an added soundtrack in the bulk of my films leaves sensorial room for the viewer-reader-audience to consider what they feel about the films and the movement it chronicles. I am also cautious about what I film and what I show. I may never show some footage because sufficient contextualization for critical and biased audiences may not be possible. In these cases, I may turn to writing instead of film, sharing with audiences in person where I can respond to them or offering insights without specifics. I avoid filming in certain cases if I feel my filming will interrupt or reveal private moments. I only film organizing and planning meetings when I am explicitly asked to.

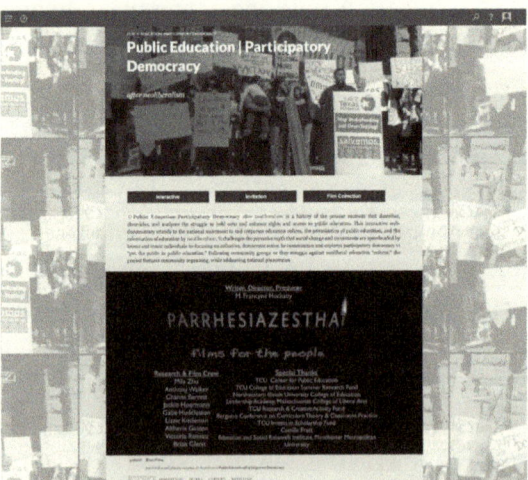

Image 6.3. *Project on Scalar*

In *Researching Resistance: Public Education After Neoliberalism* (Huckaby, forthcoming), I explore cyborg weaving in more depth. Here I focus on cyborg weaving in terms of how I weave. I want it to exist as scholarship and part of the woven tapestry of the movement. According to Haraway (2004), cyborgs weave, and this project is about weaving my machines and their human into the work of the movement to sustain, maintain, and improve neighborhood public education. While many use Haraway's (2004) cyborg theory for resistance and survival, often forgotten is the cyborg's need for connection through affinity, coalition, and political kinship—to transform border wars into "pleasure in the confusion of boundaries" (p. 8). Cyborg weaving is such a confusion in the borders of difference. Cyborgs, unlike multinational corporations and computer systems, do not network. They weave. Networking connects one thing to other multiple one things, which in turn connect to other multiple ones. In weaving, one thing (threads and fibers called the warp) rests along other such things, while another thing (a thread called woof) positions above and under, over, and through the series of parallel fibers that form the warp. Weaving builds fabric, textiles, and tapestries—stuff for making things. Networking builds networks. If one line in a network breaks, then that connection is severed. However, if a fiber woven breaks, then the cloth holds.

Becoming a scholar-cyborg who is part of the movement has meant that I weave myself into the movement by visiting sites of resistance, getting to know the people of the movement, studying their activism and movement-building work, and then sharing my work with them. Therefore, I must make my work accessible to the viewer-reader-audiences beyond academia. To make this project public or *pŭblicāre* (to use the Latin), using multiple genres has meant identifying methods for establishing credibility, recognition, and respect for my work beyond the typical mechanisms established for manuscripts, such as peer review and warranting via book publishers. This project needed to be open access so that people could easily engage it. I also chose this route to avoid the pressures that film distribution and sales demand, mainly creating films that would appeal to a large enough audience. Such a route can establish credibility, but it can also limit access for people without resources to host film screenings, purchase access online, buy DVDs, or subscribe to the various TV and film channels. For these reasons, I host the project titled *Public Education|Participatory Democracy After Neoliberalism*, online through Scalar at scalar.usc.edu/works/publiceducation.

Scalar is an open access platform for authoring and publishing born-digital media-rich scholarship. A model for 21st-century scholarly communication, Scalar explores new genres for scholarship and paradigms for publication and warranting scholarship. Created by the Alliance for Networking Visual Culture (ANVC) and funded by the Andrew W. Mellon Foundation and the National Endowment for the Humanities, Scalar is a viable publishing experiment. Scalar allows for nonlinear navigation of my digital work and the integration of film, media, and text, as Lewis (2004) recommends.

Scalar makes this project available to academics and community members. To craft the online design to the needs of diverse viewer-reader-audiences, I developed a navigation architecture that allows for multiple routes through the project's content and learned some basic coding during the summer 2017 Humanities Intensive Learning and Teaching workshop on Scalar led by ANVC's Curtis Fletcher. (I still need to review my notes and cheat sheets whenever I make coding adaptations to the project.) At the time I developed the architecture of my site, I utilized pages, paths, tags, annotations, and media functions.[3] On the pages I placed content (i.e., film, text, images) for the project and collected related pages with paths to create clusters of content. On the pages with content, I added tags to create pop-up windows with additional content for highlighted objects on a page. I also used annotations primarily on the films. Through coding, I added clickable buttons that allow for navigation between the page clusters. I was pleased that through Scalar I created a website that allowed viewer-reader-audiences to navigate as they wished without getting lost. I did find one frustration difficult to solve. I wanted quick and easy movement between individual films on a page and the collection of films overall so that a visitor to the site did not have to move through all of the pages and paths to view the collection of films or a specific film. I eventually developed a mechanism by adding an annotation to each individual film that linked to a collection of shorts and extended play films (Image 6.4).

Public Education|Participatory Democracy After Neoliberalism weaves film-text, historical-present, and practical-theoretical to describe, chronicle, and analyze the struggle to hold onto and enhance rights and access to public education. Because I want this interactive site to reach a broad base of viewer-reader-audiences, I write text and produce short films in ways that are accessible and hold onto the complexity of the ideas I share. I do not shy away from theory because nonacademics will visit the site. Instead, I work to write

Cyborg Scholarship: Films for the People 113

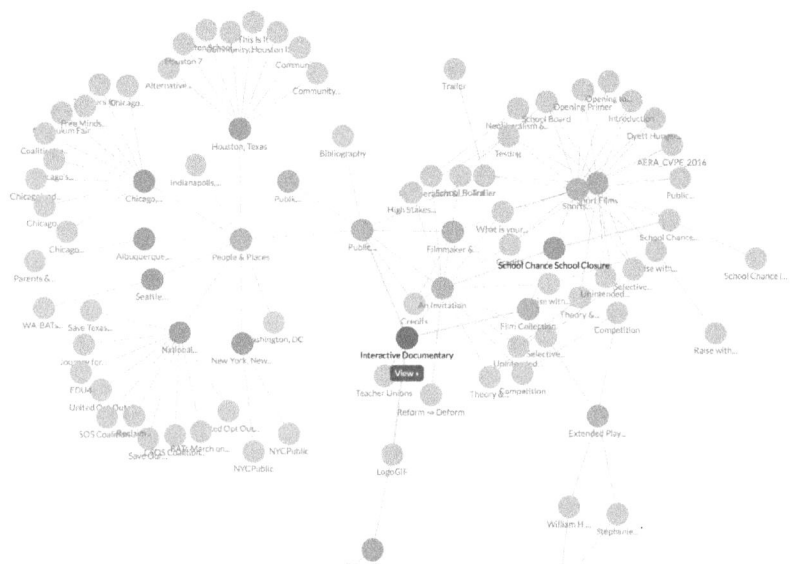

Image 6.4. *Architecture of site on Scalar*

theory in ways that are accessible to students, teachers, parents, grandparents, and community members. One way I accomplish this task is to test my text and films as multimedia presentations and screenings with live audiences and then revise given their feedback before *pūblicāre* on Scalar. Crafting shorts and presentations for diverse audiences forces me to write and produce in ways that are accessible and yet hold onto the complexity of the ideas I want to share. For example, I gave a multimedia presentation on the project followed by a 45-minute cut screened during lunch at the Community Voices for Public Education's Educational Forum (November 21, 2015). The presentation was my first public sharing and testing of my use of Haraway's (2004) cyborg theory and Lorde's (2009) necessity of poetry. The audience responded with a series of questions and comments that led me to further develop this work by explicating more clearly what I meant by privatization, exploring further potential of Lorde and Haraway in this work, and attending to cyborg weaving more closely in my analysis, theorizing, and writing. Tom Behrman, organizer of the forum, e-mailed me after the address and film screening where I tested my use:

My test of a good sermon, lecture, or talk/ presentation is: do I take notes! The speech should be informative, convincing and inspiring. Your talk was amazing. I almost did not have enough notepaper! I learned new words, good words, a new perspective and approach to the problem and was overwhelmed by your depth of knowledge and commitment, clear commitment to education and the equitable, effective teaching of our youth, and the public. You are indeed a scholar and an artist.

This unsolicited note suggested that I had found a useful way to share theory in ways that an audience of community members found engaging. Sharing scholarship with public audiences should not be a process of simplifying the scholarship or using words with fewer syllables, strategies I unfortunately still hear as solutions from fellow academics. *Pūblicāre*, instead, should be a process of becoming for academics and lay audiences, where academics introduce ideas and language in ways that facilitate understanding by community members, graciously inviting them into our conversations, and where we also learn to shed the specialized language of our work that can come across as exclusionary and elitist. Here I suggest that we work to form a hybrid-shared language for the struggle (Image 6.5).

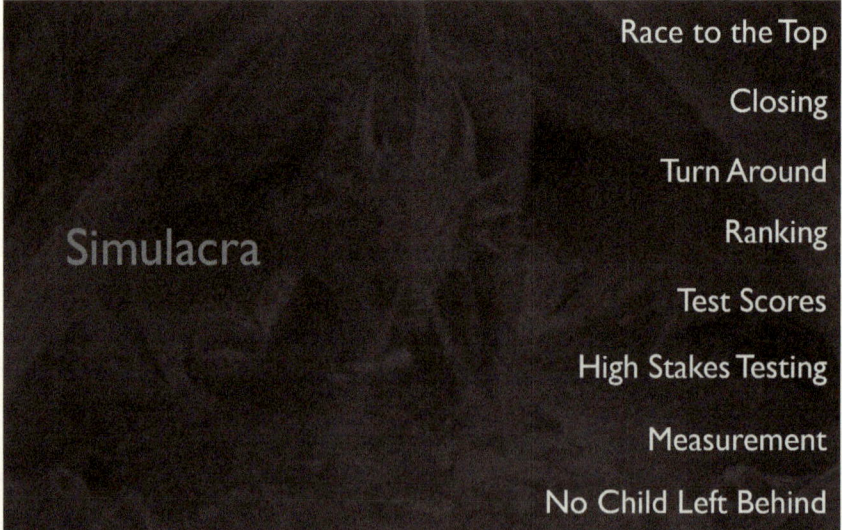

Image 6.5. *Presentation slide with words*

Cyborg Scholarship: Films for the People 115

Such an approach entailed using theoretical language with definitions, descriptions, and examples presented in lay language. As I said, words that I thought would be new for some members of the audience, I made that text appear in white, gray, or yellow letters on a dark background. I used images to illustrate the concepts, some that I created and others that I borrowed from Creative Commons. Of course, such presentations require a choreographed and well-practiced presentation. When I first began presenting this work, Mila Zhu, a doctoral student at the time, joined me to time the slides with my speaking. I have since become more proficient in working with presentations and use animation and timing functions to pair images and written text with my spoken words. I also included images of book covers alongside written quotations that I shared so that people would know the sources and could read along with me. My goal with these strategies is to create a space that brushes aside the divides and barriers that too easily find ground between academics and communities, the towns and the gown (Image 6.6).

Image 6.6. *Notations for pairing screened presentation with spoken words*

Following Lorde's (2009) lead, I wrote and interspersed poetry. For example, to share my perspective about the importance of poetry and the inspiration Lorde provides, I transition from prose to spoken word as I explore Lorde's work:

> there's something about Audre Lorde
> something about the way she writes
> that she—teaches
> invites settling into places, quieting into possibility
> learning to be
> learning to learn from there
> it's not not silent, not a place of silence
> but a quieting that's necessary
> a quiet to hear, a whisper, to feel

One of the poems I wrote first for such a presentation, "Grassroots Pedagogy" (Huckaby, 2016), is now published in a special issue on pedagogies of resistance and survivance. This work is my attempt to address Lorde's (2009) questions: "How do we deal across our differences of community, time, place and history? In other words, how do we learn to love each other while we are embattled on so many fronts?" (p. 94). The visualization of words, spoken word, images, examples, and films of various lengths offers different routes for sharing ideas and invites audiences into coming to know the ideas and experiences I share in a variety of ways.

Cyborg Scholarship and the Struggle

Scholarly filmmaking as a form of arts-based inquiry understands the "power of form to inform" (Eisner; cited in Finely, 2005, p. 681). As Finely (2005) notes, it is rooted in understanding social science as moral and political. This work is my contribution to the struggle. Through this work I have woven myself into the struggle. This work is amplification, listening to understand, learn, and share. I enact intersectional feminist theorizing to not just think about, but to feel into the details of fine threads and the beautiful tapestry the collective struggle weaves. This is a tapestry that has shaped this project and this scholar-cyborg; indeed, we would not exist as we do without the movement. I am not talking about superficial feelings, what Ming Fang He (personal communication 2016) calls pathetic feelings, but deeper feelings that can open us to a willingness to understand in the borders. This is a form of heuristic filmmaking (Lewis, 2004). This is Black feminist scholarship. This is about survival. These are films for the people.

1 Karen Lewis, the president of the Chicago Teachers Union, shared these questions in her talk at the United Opt Out Occupy the DOE 2.0 in 2013.
2 I avoided conducting this study in the city where I live and work, Fort Worth, Texas. I did not know what people would experience and express. By excluding Fort Worth and the surrounding cities from the study, I did not have to worry about the conflicts that could arise with studying the communities of the school districts that worked in collaboration with my university. This choice offered me the freedom to be more honest with my writing.
3 Updates and modifications occur on Scalar regularly that may provide options different from the ones I describe.

References

Arendt, H. (1961). *Between past and future: Six exercises in political thought.* New York, NY: Viking.
Atwood, M. (1986). *The handmaid's tale.* New York, NY: Houghton Mifflin Harcourt.
Baudrillard, J. (1983). *Simulations.* New York, NY: Simiotext[e].
Bergman, R. (Producer), & Frakes, J. (Director). (1996). *Star Trek: First contact* [Motion picture]. Los Angeles, CA: Paramount Pictures.
Bogard, W. (1987). Sociology in the absence of the social: The significance of Baudrillard for contemporary thought. *Philosophy and Social Criticism, 13*(3), 227-242.
Bourdieu, P., Sapiro, G., & McHale, B. (1991). First lecture: Social space and symbolic space: Introduction to a Japanese reading of distinction. *Poetics Today, 12*(4), 627-638.
Bourdieu, P., & Wacquant, L. J. D. (1992). *An invitation to reflexive sociology.* Chicago, IL: University of Chicago Press.
Brown v. Board of Education, 347 U.S. 483 (1954).
Castro, A. (2011, May 25). Texas cutting $5 billion from public schools. *Huffington Post.* www.huffingtonpost.com/2011/01/19/texas-school-budget-cuts_n_811039.html.
Crawford, P. I., & Turton, D. (Eds.). (1992). *Film as ethnography.* Manchester, UK: Manchester University Press.
del Conte, J., & Hornberger, D. (Directors). (2014). *Standardized lies, money & civil rights: How testing is ruining public education* [Motion picture]. Reading, PA: Rockfish Productions.

Finely, S. (2005). Arts-based inquiry: Performing revolutionary pedagogy. In N. K. Denzin & Y. S. Lincoln (Eds.), *The Sage handbook of qualitative research* (3rd ed., pp. 681–694). Thousand Oaks, CA: Sage.

Foucault, M. (1997). The ethics of the concern for self as practice of freedom. In P. Rabinow (Ed.), *Michel Foucault: Ethics, subjectivity and truth* (Vol. 1, pp. 281-302). New York, NY: The New Press.

Foucault, M. (2008). *The birth of biopolitics: Lectures at the College de France, 1978-79*. London, UK: Palgrave MacMillan

Giroux, H. (2008). *Against the terror of neoliberalism: Politics beyond the age of greed*. Boulder, CO: Paradigm.

Grumet, M. (1988). *Bitter milk: Women and teaching*. Herat, MA: University of Massachusetts Press.

Guinier, L., & Torres, G. (2003). *The miner's canary: Enlisting race, resisting power, transforming democracy*. Cambridge, MA: Harvard University Press.

Haraway, D. (1991). *Simians, cyborgs, and women: The reinvention of nature*. New York, NY: Routledge.

Haraway, D. (2004). A manifesto for cyborgs: Science, technology, and socialist feminism in the 1980s. In *The Haraway reader* (pp. 7-45). New York, NY: Routledge.

Huckaby, M. F. (Producer & Director). (2015). *Public education: Participatory democracy after neoliberalism* [Video file]. Fort Worth, TX: Parrhesiazesthai.

Huckaby, M. F. (2016). Grassroots pedagogy [Pedagogies of Resistance and Survivance special issue]. *Equity and Excellence in Education, 49*(4), 402.

Huckaby, M. F. (2017). Becoming cyborg: Activist filmmaker, the living camera, participatory democracy, and their weaving. *International Review of Qualitative Research, 10*(4), 340-359.

Huckaby, M. F. (Myers Education Press, Forthcoming). *Researching Resistance: Public Education After Neoliberalism*.

Koro-Ljungberg, M., & Cannella, G. S. (2017). Critical qualitative inquiry: Histories, methodologies, and possibilities. *International Review of Qualitative Research, 10*(4), 327-339.

Kumashiro, K. K. (2012). *Bad teacher: How blaming teachers distorts the bigger picture*. New York, NY: Teachers College Press.

Lather, P. (1993). Fertile obsession: Validity after poststructuralism. *The Sociological Quarterly, 34*(4), 673-693.

Lewis, E. D. (2004). From event to ethnography: Film-making and ethnographic research in Tana 'Ai, Flores, eastern Indonesia. In E. D. Lewis (Ed.), *Timothy Asch and ethnographic film* (pp. 97–122). London, UK: Routledge.

Lipman, P., & Jenkins, C. (2011). Venture philanthropy: From government to governance. In P. Lipman (Ed.), *The new political economy of urban education: Neoliberalism, race, and the right to the city* (pp. 100-119). New York, NY: Routledge.

Lorde, A. (2009). A burst of light: Living with cancer. In R. P. Byrd & B. Guy-Sheftall (Eds.), *I am your sister: Collected and unpublished writings of Audre Lorde* (pp. 81-149). New York, NY: Oxford University Press.

Martin, J. R. (1981). The ideal of the educated person. *Educational Theory, 31*(2), 97-109.

Pinar, W. F. (2004). *What is curriculum theory?* New York, NY: Routledge.

Ravitch, D. (2013). *Reign of error: The hoax of the privatization movement and the danger to America's public schools.* New York, NY: Knopf.

Rich, A. (1995). Claiming an education. In A. Rich (Ed.), *On lies, secrets, and silence: Selected prose, 1966-1978* (pp. 231-235). New York, NY: W. W. Norton.

Rouch, J. (1973). *The camera and man.* Retrieved from http://www.der.org/jean-rouch/pdf/CameraandMan-JRouch.pdf

St. Pierre, B., & Pillow, W. (Eds.). (2000). *Working the ruins: Feminist poststructural theory and methods in education.* New York, NY: Routledge.

Watkins, W. H. (2004). *The assault on public education: Confronting the politics of corporate school reform.* New York, NY: Teachers College Press.

Wood, M. (2015). Nobody puts filmmaking in a corner! *Organization Aesthetics, 4*(1), 9–11.

Section III

Strategic Next Steps and Obligations for Critical Qualitative Scholars

CHAPTER 7

The Play of Seduction and Desire in the Making of a President

Bronwyn Davies

TRUMP WAS CREATED in *The Apprentice* as a successful entrepreneur who had risen from the ashes of bankruptcy, and who not only understood the key to his own newly found success, but could teach both his audience and his participants how to live the American Dream, becoming billionaires who have started from nothing. In contrast, the big reality TV show playing in the White House is struggling to convincingly create its star performer. In this chapter, I want to explore the movement between these two shows: the first that was orchestrated so that people believed it was real, and the second, that is supposedly real, even though there are radically different interpretations of what is actually going on. I will consider the way in which audiences are seduced by fictional heroes and what part seduction has played in the movement from reality TV star in *The Apprentice* to president in the White House. I will conclude with some reflections on the implications for qualitative inquiry.

Seduction

Feminists have long since been wary of seduction, though in my experience, they are frustratingly susceptible to it. We wrote in the 1970s and 1980s about finding ourselves drawn into romantic love, even when we knew it would, more than likely, fall out badly. We marveled at the way even very old women were filled with desire for that prince who, in the end, never came (Walkerdine, 1984). Desire, we found, had a powerful emotional force, and for many of us, it had the power to override rational argument. Emotion is vital to everyday life, and even to living rationally. But it makes all of us susceptible to the false plays of appearances in seductive encounters.

In 1990, Baudrillard wrote as if he had already witnessed Trump's election with its mantra of fake news: "The capacity immanent to seduction [is] to deny things their truth and turn it into a game, the pure play of appearances, and thereby foil all systems of power and meaning with a mere turn of the hand" (p. 8). For that play of appearances to succeed, Baudrillard (1990) says, it must enchant, and enchantment "begins only after one has been taken in by one's desire" (p. 70). The play of appearances that was cultivated on *The Apprentice* lies at the heart of the Trump assemblage, and it is that dedication to the seducer's capacity to "deny things their truth" (Baudrillard, 1990, p. 8) that makes some deeply uneasy about the transformation of the reality TV star into the president.

The people who voted for Trump, in contrast, were, many of them, out of love with politics and its empty promises and its corruptions. They were, ironically, taken in by their desire for the fictional entrepreneur in *The Apprentice,* who appeared to be a truth-teller, and who appeared to know how to make America great again—to return it to being the bountiful land of milk and honey, in which anyone could rise from the ashes as Trump had done.

In Baudrillard's (1990) analysis, narcissism is the key to seduction: "Narcissus, having lost his twin sister, mourns her loss, by constituting his own face into an illusory attraction. Neither conscious nor unconscious, the dupery is fully played out and sufficient unto itself" (p. 70). And there were layers and layers of illusion and dupery going on in the production of Trump-as-star that played into the transformation into Trump-as-president. Dupery was an art Trump had long practiced as a salesman, and the Trump-as-star illusion presented him with an irresistible image that he too was seduced by. McKenzie-Murray (2017) described Trump-in-the-White House as "an eerie, modern version of the pond of Narcissus / This is our new reality. The leader of the free world is a fabulist addicted to the glow of his own image" (p. 11).

In Baudrillard's (1990) words, "To seduce is to die as reality and reconstitute oneself as illusion. It is to be taken in by one's own illusion and move in an enchanted world" (p. 69). It is that reconstitutive dynamic that I want to explore in this chapter: how Trump-as-star of *The Apprentice* was taken in by his own illusion and moved in an enchanted world. The White House has become his enchanted castle, from which he can reign supreme over a White, enchanted America.

There is probably no election that doesn't involve some play of illusions on the part of candidates and their voters. Less common, perhaps, is the transformation of a fictional character into a president. The election of Reagan, a B-movie star, was regarded with some incredulity at the time, but no one believed, as far as I know, that they were electing one of his fictional characters to the presidency. In contrast, it was the illusory Trump-as-star who captured and capitalized on the American Dream. Of course, not everyone who voted for Trump was seduced. Some were willing to give him a go, simply for the pleasure of having a comedian speaking truths that had until now been unable to be spoken in the White House. Yet others identified with and were happy to support his White male supremacist views, his belief in guns, his vulgar displays of conspicuous consumption, and his attraction to and dominance over beautiful women.

In the early 1980s, elements of the American Dream were intensified with the introduction of neoliberal government, implemented by Reagan in the United States and Prime Minister Thatcher in the United Kingdom. The guiding principles of neoliberalism were, in Thatcher's words, that "there is no such thing as society," and, further, that there is no alternative to neoliberal government. Neoliberal governments and institutions systematically made individuals more vulnerable, and hence more obedient, and pitted them against each other in the scramble to survive and to make good. Critique was concertedly undermined, as were social values. The only value that mattered was economic survival—for individuals, for institutions, and for governments. The Trump of *The Apprentice* was carefully constructed as the epitome of a neoliberal survivor, with one major difference—he would teach others how to succeed. At the same time, his own success would outstrip anyone else's.

The transformation of an illusory "reality" into a real-world event gives us a rich seam of data to work with in analyzing the plays of power that are involved in elevating someone into a position of apparently unassailable power. Rarely, perhaps never, has such a play been so transparent and made so readily accessible through social media. There are multiple research questions that could (and will) be addressed through that data. The interesting question for me here is can this transformation work in a sustained way, such that Trump-as-star might become a credible Trump-as-president?

The *Los Angeles Times* thinks not; they see a man behind the play of appearances who can never succeed:

> He is a man so unpredictable, so reckless, so petulant, so full of blind self-regard, so untethered to reality that it is impossible to know where his presidency will lead or how much damage he will do to our nation. His obsession with his own fame, wealth and success, his determination to vanquish enemies real and imagined, his craving for adulation—these traits were, of course, at the very heart of his scorched-earth outsider campaign; indeed some of them helped get him elected. But in a real presidency in which he wields unimaginable power, they are nothing short of disastrous. (The *Times* Editorial Board, 2017)

That description of Trump as obsessed with his own fame, wealth, and success, and as determined to vanquish his enemies, is the description of someone successfully transformed into the competitive, individualistic subject of neoliberalism without social values, the very kind of subject our institutions and governments have been pressing us all to become (Davies, 2018; Davies, Somerville, & Claiborne, 2017).

From Illusory Star to President

Before release, reality TV shows are edited to retrospectively produce a convincing script. The storylines the viewer sees may bear no relation to what actually happened during production. What the audience sees on screen is not a "natural" or spontaneous unfolding of events, but a magic bringing together of fragments to create an illusion that is intended to seduce its audience not only into believing that the constructed narrative is a straightforward representation of what happened, but also to becoming emotionally involved in the fortunes of the participants. To create the show, the participants play out a variety of semi-structured scenarios, and out of the multiple fragments and possible storylines, the "real" story is produced.

In the big reality show in the White House, the celebrity star seems to have fired the director, and the raw footage is being released before the script writers have had a chance to work on it. Chaotic and risky as that may seem to be, that is what a lot of people love about Trump. Unlike other politicians who infuriate everyone with the mindless repetitions of their scripted lines, he appears to be real, which is more important to them than any mistake he might make. What his admirers hear in what Trump-the-president offers is what he offered in *The Apprentice*—not just the means of survival but the means of succeeding in a competitive neoliberal world.

The transformation of Trump-as-star to Trump-as-president who is running a show in the White House (as he has instructed his aides to think of each day being) has generated global fascination. The chaotic stream of words and events has led, and continues to lead, to multiple guesses as to which storyline is actually being played out. For some of his supporters, the chaotic utterances and impulsive tweets are evidence of a refreshingly real person in the presidency. Yet other supporters find a kindred spirit who shares both their language and their aspirations.

Critics are more likely to be confounded, and to go on endlessly wondering how the multiple fragments and scenarios might come together in an account that makes sense—an account that might come to be regarded as the truth of the Trump presidency. Could the United States of America cease to be united? Those states, which have held onto some semblance of pride in what the nation once believed it stood for, could break away and become independent nations. Such collapses can and do happen. Or will there be a revolution sparked by the #metoo movement? Or perhaps it will end in a grand conflagration. Goldberg expressed that fear when in December 2017 he wrote, "The world right now is a powder keg. Trump, an untethered maniac, sits atop it, flicking a lighter that Republicans in Congress could take away, but won't. If everything goes up in flames, we can't say we weren't warned." And Malbon (2017) earlier wrote, with deep concern:

> Though we have mechanisms for removing a dangerous president, those mechanisms are too politically explosive to actually invoke. President Trump could order a nuclear holocaust before breakfast, but unless society can agree that he is either criminal or comatose, both America and the world are stuck with him and all the damage he can cause.

The storyline that many of his detractors hope to wake up to is that Trump-as-president has realized he has been getting his lines wrong, and has begun to figure how it is that you "do" president. He realizes he has to listen to his advisors, just as he listened to the producers of *The Apprentice*. His advisors, however, appear to despair of any such transformation taking place (Haberman, Thrush, & Baker, 2017). Malbon commented, in November 2017,

> Of late I have been asking Republicans who work either in the White House or closely with it whether Trump is learning on the job—whether he is becoming more judicious, more disciplined, more serious. The answer, unanimously, is that he is not. He is the man he was the day he stepped into the Oval Office, the same man he was on the campaign trail, the same man so many of us feared he would be as President.

And so the speculation continues as to how the storyline in this big show will unfold. Perhaps the actions Trump engages in will eventually lead to his undoing. Some of those who envisage an impeachment scenario also discuss the possibility that the sense that will be made of the unpredictable chaos is that Trump is mad. Or much more scarily, and perhaps more plausibly, some guess that what appears as mad or infantile will actually be revealed as Machiavellian machinations that are aimed at a total takeover of power in the name of the alt-right and of White male supremacy, leading to the end of democracy as we know it, and quite probably to nuclear war.

The trouble with such speculations is that the outcomes they envisage are, for many, too frightening. The temptation is to switch off, and return to their ordinary lives, where they can depend on the sun rising each morning onto ordinary days, and setting each evening into safe, ordinary nights, in which the world as we know it has the power to continue. For some, that ordinary life, though, has been shattered by the foreclosures on their houses and the demise of manufacturing, and they want to believe the promise that their life can be restored.

The thrill of immersion in the illusory play of appearances isn't thrilling anymore if the storyline gets too scary. For those who have the possibility of return to an ordinary life, there is comfort in the belief that it is all really under control, and that the scaremongering is just fake news that can be ignored. The Republicans can be trusted, they hope, just as the sun can be trusted to rise, to know what they are doing. Believing in and trusting the president and the government to know what they are doing offers an escape from the pervasive vulnerability that everyone is subjected to under neoliberalism (Butler, 2004). Even Trump feels vulnerable in the face of his poor ratings and the negative press he receives.

The *Access Hollywood* Tape

A Deleuzian method for gaining insight into complex assemblages such as the Trump assemblage is to begin with a concrete case, which enables you to come close to the movement of thought as it unfolds: "the starting point required by Deleuze's method is always a concrete case ... [Y]ou place yourself where thought has already started, as close as possible to a singular case and to the movement of thought" (Badiou, 2002, p. 13). And that singular case is made out of the "generative flux of forces and relations that work to produce particular realities" (Deleuze & Guattari, 2004, p. 7). The singular documented case I turn to, then, is the conversation on the bus in which Trump boasted about his predatory sexual molestation of women.

The *Access Hollywood* tape, as transcribed by Penn Bullock of the *New York Times* (2016), recorded Trump talking to Billy Bush and seven other men on the set of *Days of Our Lives,* where he was to make a cameo appearance:

Donald J. Trump: You know and ...

Unknown: She used to be great. She's still very beautiful.

Trump: I moved on her, actually. You know, she was down on Palm Beach. I moved on her, and I failed. I'll admit it.

Unknown: Whoa.

Trump: I did try and fuck her. She was married.

Unknown: That's huge news.

Trump: No, no, Nancy. No, this was [unintelligible]—and I moved on her very heavily. In fact, I took her out furniture shopping. She wanted to get some furniture. I said, "I'll show you where they have some nice furniture." I took her out furniture—I moved on her like a bitch. But I couldn't get there. And she was married. Then all of a sudden I see her, she's now got the big phony tits and everything. She's totally changed her look...

Trump: Yeah, that's her. With the gold. I better use some Tic Tacs just in case I start kissing her. You know, I'm automatically attracted to beautiful—I just start kissing them. It's like a magnet. Just kiss. I don't even wait. And when you're a star, they let you do it. You can do anything.

Bush: Whatever you want.

Trump: Grab 'em by the pussy. You can do anything... [they arrive at their destination]

Bush: Down below, pull the handle.

Trump: Hello, how are you? Hi!

Arianne Zucker: Hi, Mr. Trump. How are you? Pleasure to meet you.

Trump: Nice seeing you. Terrific, terrific. You know Billy Bush?

Bush: Hello, nice to see you. How you doing, Arianne?

Zucker: Doing very well, thank you. Are you ready to be a soap star?

Trump: We're ready, let's go. Make me a soap star.

Bush: How about a little hug for the Donald? He just got off the bus.

Zucker: Would you like a little hug, darling?

Trump: O.K., absolutely. Melania said this was O.K.

The conversation was accompanied by continuous and explosive laughter from the eight men who were with Trump on the bus. Their repeated guffaws egged him on. They were not simply laughing because they found what he said to be funny. Each was paid substantial money to gratify Trump-as-star, who had become a television cash cow.

Yet the laughter was not simply fake laughter. The outrageousness of Trump's talk has the same effect that comedians have when they dare to make taboo statements. When comedians say things that people in everyday life don't dare to say, the audience collectively bursts into laughter, not necessarily believing what is said, but loving the rush of energy that comes when someone engages in flagrant rule-breaking and gets away with it. Further, as Berlant and Ngai (2017) point out, the ones who laugh are personally implicated in the desire for (and the shame of) what is being revealed:

> In the comedic scene things are always closer to each other than they appear. They are near each other in a way that prompts a disturbance in the air. People can enjoy that disturbance, and one thing they can enjoy in it is that it feels automatic, spontaneous, freed-up. Pressed a little, the enjoyment is not always, hardly ever, unmixed; but in the moment, the feeling of freedom exists with its costliness. There's a relation between the grin and chagrin; there's the fatigue from feeling vulnerable because pleasure's bad objects are not always in one's control. (p. 248)

What part did that complicity play in the creation of the Trump-as-president assemblage? Had Trump fallen into the trap that many celebrities are wary of—believing in what their audiences see, even when they are aware of the artifice and of the role of others in putting "lipstick on the pig," as Schwartz described his own role in ghostwriting *The Art of the Deal* (Trump & Schwartz, 1987; Winsor, 2016). Did Billy Bush, Schwartz, and incidental players like Arianne Zucker create Trump-as-star so successfully that he lost sight of the fact that his stardom was based on an intricate web of deception?

The moment Trump began thinking out loud, in his Trump-as-star manifestation, of running for president, he began seriously blurring for himself the line between the concocted illusion, for which he was paid a great deal of money, and the truth of himself. I'm not talking about big T-truth here, or about an essential self that Trump might be thought to possess. I am talking about a truth of himself as something not based on *calculated* deception and falsehood. All "truth of oneself" is to some extent illusory.

What the men on the bus with Trump later said was that they didn't realize that Trump was telling the truth about his sexual predations; they thought it was just one more deception, one more comedic revelation of their own sexual desires. They didn't know they were rewarding him for bragging about the abusive power he routinely exerted over women, a power that he believed was in his nature: "You know, I'm automatically attracted to beautiful—I just start kissing them. It's like a magnet. Just kiss. I don't even wait."

When first confronted with the tape, Trump lightly dismissed it as "locker room talk" that had happened a long time ago; it was nothing more than boys being boys. When there was uproar among the Republicans, he apologized: "Anyone who knows me knows these words don't reflect who I am," he said. "I said it, I was wrong, and I apologize" (Burns, Haberman, & Martin, 2016). He was making a claim, then, that he did have an essential nature, and it was not in that nature to molest women "automatically," as he had claimed on the bus.

When a number of women came forward to say the bragging was based on fact, and that he had sexually assaulted them, he dismissed them as liars. When the #metoo movement erupted, and men began losing their jobs as a result of women's revelations, Trump changed his story, claiming, "We don't think that is my voice" (Haberman & Martin, 2017). He is not, of course, the first American president to deny his sexual predations, though he is perhaps the first to give rise to such a powerful feminist uprising against the sexual predations of men in power.

Malbon (2017) commented in response to Trump's denial: "it is unclear whether Trump is lying to us, or if he is somehow lying to himself, as well. And it is hard to say which would be scarier." Goldberg (2017) puts it another way: "There is a debate over whether Trump is unaware of reality or merely indifferent to it. He might be delusional, or he might simply be asserting the power to blithely override the truth, which is the ultimate privilege of the despot." It is impossible, as yet, to know which is the correct reading—madness, or the birth of a despot. What is clear is that the play with truth is dangerous, harnessing as it does the anger and insecurity that have been so magnified under neoliberal forms of governance:

> The insult that Donald Trump brings to the equation is an apparent disregard for fact so profound as to suggest that he may not see much practical distinction between lies, if he believes they serve him, and the truth... He targets the darkness, anger and insecurity that hide in each of us and harnesses them for his own purposes. If one of his lies doesn't work—well, then he lies about that. (The *Times* Editorial Board, 2017b)

Trump's profound disregard for facts is long-standing. When Bush chided him for inflating his TV ratings, Trump explained that it was okay to lie, because people are gullible: "People will just believe you. You just tell them and they believe you" (Bush, 2017).

Billy Bush's response to Trump's denial that it was his voice on the tape was published as an op-ed piece in the *New York Times* titled "Billy Bush: Yes, Donald Trump, You Said That." The eight men laughed, he said, because they thought it was just another facet of the dupery they were all engaged in; Trump's words were "hypothetical hot air from America's highest-rated bloviator" (a bloviator being someone who engages in a style of empty, pompous speech that goes on for a long time and says nothing). They thought, he wrote, that it was a "crass stand-up act" and that Trump was performing for laughs. So they gave him the laughs he wanted. "Surely, we thought, none of this was real." But as Berlant and Ngai (2017) point out, they were also complicit in their laughter, setting aside any values that might have prohibited such collusion in imagined scenarios of male predation.

In Bush's account of that collusion, he found himself, in some profound personal sense, undone, when he read the first-hand accounts of the women who had, in real life, been molested by the predatory Trump-as-star. The conversation on the bus was no longer stand-up comedy, but an act through which he, Billy Bush, lost part of his own soul. His coimplication in the pussy-grabbing saga now appears in all its shame. He is outraged at Trump's denial, when the "country is currently trying to reconcile itself to years of power abuse and sexual misconduct" and when men like Billy Bush feel shame and remorse for the part they have played in the making of Trump-as-star:

> The key to succeeding in my line of work was establishing a strong rapport with celebrities. I did that, and was rewarded for it. My segments with Donald Trump when I was just a correspondent were part of the reason I got promoted. NBC tripled my salary and paid for my moving van from New York to Los Angeles. Was I acting out of self-interest? You bet I was. Was I alone? Far from it. With Mr. Trump's outsized viewership back in 2005, everybody from Billy Bush on up to the top brass on the 52nd floor had to stroke the ego of the big cash cow along the way to higher earnings. None of us were guilty of knowingly enabling our future president. But all of us were guilty of sacrificing a bit of ourselves in the name of success. (Bush, 2017)

That bit of himself was the bit of humanity that neoliberalism sought, and still seeks, to expunge (Davies & Bansel, 2005).

Billy Bush and the other seven men on the bus are not alone in being seduced by power and by stardom, and of exploiting it as a means to further their own success. Their seduction is part of an entanglement in stardom and power that is at work in capitalist countries everywhere; it is a seduction, as Bush says, that might destroy your own soul, and ultimately your nation.

And so...

How might we, as part of the audience to this big show, find a way to contribute to this event in a way that matters and makes a difference? Some of us have given up imagining there will ever be a coherent storyline that emerges. The only hope is that the show will fold altogether when Trump's followers fall off even further, and he has no viable base left. Perhaps it will have a natural ending, requiring no effort. There is a degree of slothfulness in any democracy...

But disbelief and the mantra of fake news can be powerful tools in the hands of a Machiavellian leader. Hard truths have to be examined in careful detail, not just so we can say they are bad and must stop, but so we can understand how they happen and how we are implicated in them. None of us is immune to being seduced or to being caught up in collective desires. To counter seduction, we need to examine our own vulnerability to seduction—and not blame others for being duped while assuming ourselves to be above and apart from cultural entanglements. Our challenges here are to understand how desire and seduction are at work, to understand the negative press of neoliberal thought and practice, and to understand the history and the politics of the current situation.

The world has rarely been so much in need of people who can think hard about what's going on. Swamped by social media, confused by our own desires, including the desire not to know, we collectively depend on, and must ourselves become, those who can think their way through the quagmire of power, illusion, desire, and seduction—not casting those others who love what Trump does as other and alien, but seeing them as entangled in the same contradictory set of forces and entanglements as we all are.

Neoliberal governments are antagonistic to the kinds of critique we social scientists are capable of. We can't expect praise from government or its institutions for such critique, though our survival depends in part on such praise. As neoliberal subjects, it is difficult to engage in work that is disruptive; it takes courage, strong collegial support, and an unwavering collective desire for a better future.

References

Badiou, A. (2002). *Ethics: An essay on the understanding of evil* (Peter Hallward, Trans.). London, UK: Verso.
Baudrillard, J. (1990). *Seduction* (M. Singer, Trans.). New York, NY: St. Martin's Press.
Berlant, L., & Ngai, S. (2017). Comedy has issues. *Critical Inquiry, 43*(2), 233-249.
Bush, B. (2017, April 12). Billy Bush: Yes, Donald Trump, you said that. *The New York Times*.
Butler, J. (2004). *Precarious life. The powers of mourning and violence*. London, UK: Verso.
Burns, A., Haberman, M., & Martin, J. (2016, October 7). Donald Trump apology caps day of outrage over lewd tape. *The New York Times*.
Davies, B. (2018, May). *Seduction and desire: The power of spectacle*. International Congress of Qualitative Inquiry keynote address, Urbana, IL.
Davies, B., & Bansel, P. (2005). The time of their lives? Academic workers in neoliberal time(s). *Health Sociology Review, 14*(1), 47-58.
Davies, B., Somerville, M., & Claiborne, L. (2017). Feminist poststructuralisms and the neoliberal university. In N. K. Denzin & M. D. Giardina (Eds.), *Qualitative inquiry in neoliberal times* (pp. 87-103). New York, NY: Routledge.
Deleuze, G., & Guattari, F. (2004). *A thousand plateaus: Capitalism and schizophrenia* (B. Massumi, Trans.). London, UK: Continuum.

Goldberg, M. (2017, December 1). Trump is cracking up. *The New York Times*.

Haberman, M., & Martin, J. (2017, November 28). Trump once said the "Access Hollywood" tape was real. Now he's not sure. *The New York Times*.

Haberman, M., Thrush, G., & Baker, P. (2017, December 9). Inside Trump's hour-by-hour battle for self-preservation. *The New York Times*.

Malbon, C. (2017, November 30). The case for normalizing impeachment. *Vox*.

McKenzie-Murray, M. (2017, March 11-17). Battle him of the Republic. *The Saturday Paper*, pp. 1, 10-11.

The *New York Times*. (2016, October 8). Transcript: Donald Trump's taped comments about women. Retrieved from https://www.nytimes.com/2016/10/08/us/donald-trump-tape-transcript.html?_r=0

The *Times* Editorial Board. (2017a, April 2). Our dishonest president. *Los Angeles Times*.

The *Times* Editorial Board. (2017b, April 3). Why Trump lies. *Los Angeles Times*.

Trump, D., & Schwartz, T. (1987). *The art of the deal*. New York, NY: Random House.

Walkerdine, V. (1984). Some day my prince will come. In A. McRobbie & M. Nava (Eds.), *Gender and generation*. London, UK: Macmillan.

Winsor, M. (2016, July 18). Tony Schwartz, co-author of Donald Trump's "The Art of the Deal," says Trump presidency would be "terrifying.'" ABC News. Retrieved from http://abcnews.go.com/US/tony-schwartz-author-donald-trumps-art-deal-trump/story?id=40662196

CHAPTER 8

Nurturing Our Critical Relations
Research to Facilitate Justice Through Postanthropocentric Transformation

Gaile S. Cannella

AS HAS BECOME clear to almost everyone, we are now required to deal directly with a world in which misogyny, extreme racism, ultranationalism, and crony capitalism reign, a neoliberal world in which everyone is judged by their ability to generate money (and/or perpetuate the capitalist con), a world in which White, gendered backlash dominates as authoritarian older men (or their puppets) are again considered saviors, strong, and smart because they know how to break the rules, discredit others, lie, and win the game. Even as movements such as Black Lives Matter (n.d.) gain attention and some prominence, in this contemporary right-wing, antidemocratic, uncaring, crazy, and increasingly fascist circumstance (at least in the United States), women, people of color, youth, the poor, immigrants, the elderly, and even intellectuals who would dare speak truth to power face increased objectification, silencing, hatred, and violence. An unfortunate but profound example reported by the U.S. Federal Bureau of Investigation (FBI) is that hate crimes increased by 5% in 2016, with the major increase being toward Muslims (Bayoumi, 2018; Lopez, 2017). Further, lives of all living creatures, as well as the earth, are placed in great peril. Violence against protected species, all others, and the environment increases at warp speed as regulations are being eliminated, information sites censored, and green environmental plans scraped (National Geographic, 2018).

For at least 30 years, most critical scholars have created research projects grounded in the belief that we could work to counter injustice. Yet, just transformations have not always been the result. Reasons why have been discussed, ranging from academic isolation and elitism in language to Euro-Western male domination to corporate capitalism. More attention is needed regarding this range of reasons, as well as related actions that could/should be taken. However, we now also know that we have underestimated the impacts of (a) neoliberal all-invasive capitalist patriarchy (and the variety of rapidly developing technologies and efficiencies associated with it, ranging from medical body surveillance devices—to Facebook—to smart phones—to antibiotics and factory farms), and (b) the reactions of human beings who have been unable to accept diversity, challenges to their own truths, or their own perceived loss of power. These underestimations explain much of our current condition. Our reactions, research, and actions to counter these complexities must begin to always take them into account.

Therefore, in this current context, in these troubled times, and to determine possibilities for direct action, I want to propose that we nurture our present and future connections and relations with the multiplicities of critical histories. Further, these critical histories can becomewith (Haraway, 2016) both our critical presents and futures to yield previously unthought entangled bodies, agents, and events toward a more just world. To illustrate the meaning of becomingwith in troubled times, Haraway (2016) employs what most would call a posthuman[1] perspective as she states, "Staying with the troubles requires making oddkin; that is we require each other in unexpected collaborations and combinations, in hot compost piles" (p. 4).

Haraway (2016) uses constructs like oddkin, critters, and making-with, as well as becomingwith, where (stating that becoming is not really a relation) companions or partners (whether alive or not) are constituted through intra- and interaction (which she takes from Barad, 2007). Becomingswith are unexpected combinations and collaborations, nurturing relations that loop around and through one another. Becomingswith are how partners are rendered capable (Haraway, 2016). Becomingwith is an excellent postanthropocentric perspective that can be entangled with and nurturing of critical histories and transformative action. For consideration here, I choose to use the concept in the plural because all people, histories, oddkin, critters, ideas, and actions are involved in multiplicities and unpredictabilities. Further, the construct can embody both namings and actions simultaneously.

This nurturing requires us to consider history and relations that can emerge by entangling our concerns for a more just and equitable world with traditional critical inquiry and recent research perspectives that are often labeled posthuman. The reader is reminded that much of what is often labeled traditional critical inquiry can actually be considered broader than views that privilege the human, especially when postcolonial, indigenous, and feminist of color knowledges are rightfully included as they have historically gone beyond the human. The focus of this chapter is therefore to consider how these immanent entangled relations can be considered potential locations for counteraction regarding the multiple and increasing injustices that affect various groups of people as well as their more-than-human companions (whether so-called domesticated or wild) and the environments within which we all live. To accomplish this purpose, I stress the importance of historical critical research and knowledges (currently often denied) for both problematizations of and actions in the present, as well as to make obvious the work over many years of philosophical perspectives and actions by critical scholars often in conjunction with community activists in the name of political activism and transformations toward a more just world.

My philosophical biases and concerns for research purposes, resistance, and action continue to be embedded within my interpretations of postcolonial critique, decolonialism/anticolonialism (L. Gandhi, 1998; Mohanty, 1988; Said, 1978; Spivak, 1988), Foucault's (1997, 2003) genealogy, as well as genealogy of critique (Folkers, 2016), the work of scholars of color from diverse locations and circumstances (Anzaldúa, 1987, 1990; Collins, 2000: hooks, 2000; Mohanty, 2003; Smith, 1999/2012), and feminist concerns with patriarchy and now capitalist patriarchy (Butler, 1993; Harding, 1986; von Werlhof, 2007). These views and I are becomingwith the focus of scholars who point to the human privilege in most all research, scholars such as Haraway (2008, 2016) as she challenges us to engage our connections and stay with the troubles and Wolfe (2010, 2013) as he and others have becomewith a critical animal studies that acknowledges both human as animal before the law and the precarious condition shared by all critters (whether labeled human or nonhuman) under biopolitics. Further, my bias is that broad-based injustice likely perpetuates continued human social injustice, creating a more just world requires that human actions literally intersect with concern for the more than human, and although we will probably never really be posthuman, we can continue to try.

Organizationally, to address these issues in this chapter, I first briefly overview my interpretations of critical inquiry with its multiple histories, noting research purposes and methodologies and problematizing the critique of critique historically and philosophically. Further, reminders of historical critical work and example transformations that have actually occurred are provided. Next, examples of past work historically grounded in justice broadly are included. These examples are critical work before the posthuman discussion but that go beyond privileging the human. Finally, current practices and possibilities for nurturing our critical relations and generating action literally through and within these entanglements are considered.

The Usefulness of Critical Qualitative Inquiry (CQI)

Critical qualitative inquiry can only be considered useful if one considers the multiplicities from which it has been/is generated along with the diverse, and perhaps new, forms of critique and action that can emerge from combining these multiplicities.

Multiplicities and CQI

Critical qualitative inquiry as a research perspective has emerged from a range of histories, fields, life experiences, and philosophical locations, including belief structures labeled feminisms, critical pedagogy, critical theory and poststructuralism, post/anti/decolonialism, and indigenous worldviews. These experiences and philosophical locations are multidirectional and multipurposed. Those who take action embedded within the various critical perspectives often rightfully deny similarity or affinity with each other. However, most address power relations in some form (e.g., intersections, oppression, privilege, assemblage, and contingency), whether as simplistic or complex, hierarchical or infused, deterministic or contingent—and most attempt to even avoid such dualisms while expanding opportunities for justice and equity. Critical work is grounded in the recognition of continued violence against those who are traditionally marginalized as well as centuries of struggle for gender, racial, and socioeconomic justice played out in civil wars, countercolonial actions, and persistent and prolonged social protests and public activism (Costain, 1992; Morris, 1984; Piven & Cloward, 1977; Snow, Soule, & Kriesi, 2004).

Although many conditions and perspectives literally opened doors and created necessities for critical work, the two that I mention here are the 1960s rights movements and the emergence of postmodern perspectives. First, social protests and public activisms (referenced earlier) represent a nonviolent public stand, a rising up of/by/for groups of people who had been traditionally marginalized. This activism was not new as Gandhi (2001/1951) and others took countercolonial action in India, and women around the world took action to obtain the vote as well as human rights overall (e.g., Hannam, 2005; Pankhurst, 1913/2007), just to name a few major examples. Further, Martin Luther King (1959), the leader of the 1960s civil rights movement, had traveled to India to learn from the nonviolent actions of Gandhi. So, counterforms of activism toward a more just world have emerged over centuries, have intersected, and have learned from each other. They have often becomewith before being labeled as so. However, the 1960s movements (probably along with news media technology that made action and events more immediately available to the public, as well as a few supportive politicians) made more publicly visible the diverse voices, lives, knowledges, and views of the world, as well as diverse and varied life experiences and relations that had been silenced for many generations.

This increased visibility becamewith shifts across fields such as art, literature, philosophy, and other academic disciplines in ways that challenged the existence of universal truths, especially the claims by particular groups that they were superior to others and could therefore intervene into their lives. Modernist notions of universal grand narratives, dualistic forms of interpretation (e.g., male/female, objective/subjective, right/wrong, adult/child), and human and scientific progress were revealed as cultural constructions grounded within particular dominant interpretations of the world. Although postmodernism is not the dualistic opposite of modernism (and some scholars believe that it actually reinforces and reinscribes modernism), the challenges to universals resulted in avenues for more diverse perspectives, voices, ways of thinking, and reconceptualizations of research. From within this context, major bodies of research and methodologies emerged that can be labeled critical scholarship because the work is concerned with power relations, multiplicities, and increased justice and equity (Cannella, 2015).

Critiquing Critical Inquiry

Currently, research that has revealed and challenged intersecting forms of power is under assault as without result and is not leading to more socially just transformations. Some scholars have labeled the work depressing, some calling it postpositivist, traditional, or conventional, and some even labeling this critical work that would reveal power and inequities as "running out of steam" (Latour, 2004). This critique of past critical work as currently accepted and used by many actually perpetuates dualisms, enlightenment linear views of academic and social progress, oversimplifications, and human privilege (that, in my understanding, the "critique of critique" would have hoped to counter). Further, academic debates and conversations abound, such as research suggesting that Latour's (2004) interpretations of the postcolonial critique has ignored and does not understand cultural meanings in that literature (Ray & Selinger, 2008), Noys's (2011) problematizations of the notion of affirmation within which we can problematize the interpretation of critique as dualistic (whether affirmation or negation), or reminders that Foucault's genealogies can be considered events that become ways to actually limit the power of dominant forms of reason (Folkers, 2016). These genealogies are about more than how facts become matters of concern (Latour, 2004), but rather if certain matters should be of concern—"the politics of truth" (Foucault, 1997)—for example, if educational equity should be a matter of concern. Further, critical scholarship is not always critique, and all forms of critique are not the same. Hopefully, these basics are enough to remind us of the complexity within which our critical work is employed academically.

Critical work has been transformative, whether in the lives of, for example, mothers who come to understand that there are multiple ways to support their children or same-sex partners who are now accepted as forming families together. However, many groups of human beings are still suffering—living in poverty—tested and labeled—deported—treated as if their cultures and languages are not of any value—are displaced and marginalized—are suffering and dying. Further, the well-being of those who are not labeled human is literally ignored by most. Critical work and scholarship have by no means run out of steam. Rather, we live in such complex and power-oriented conditions (brought on by particular groups of self-identified human beings) that critical work has never been more important and so must be continued and expanded. Further, living within this global context that perpetuates inequities, injustices, and suffering while attempting to erase and disqualify past critical work, those of us who are concerned with increased justice (social, environmental, or otherwise) must continue to ask and plan: What do we do next? What are the multiple actions that can be taken? How do we becomewith? How do we think, act, and be what we have never imagined?

Acknowledging Critical Becomingswith Histories

To answer these questions, I would always want to acknowledge and employ the critical work that has emerged historically and the possibilities for expanding the usefulness of that work. Further, dismissing that work as elitist or too narrow erases a range of resources that are much needed in both the present and future if we are to increase justice and fairness broadly. More important, erasure negates the voices and work of many women and people of color over the past several decades, another form of continued sexism and racism (Jackson, 2015). This work has engaged with diverse realities, revolutionary ethics, unthought relations, and direct actions in the attempt to increase justice. We can definitely find historical time periods, events, actions, critiques, thoughts, and beings where oddkin and unexpected and previously unthought collaborations and understandings have emerged as direct challenges to unjust power relations. Critical perspectives do have becomingswith histories, even before being given a name. Unfortunately, human injustice remains, and the more than human, the environment, and the earth have not been equitably involved agents in most of these becomingswith.

Human beings have been at the center of most critical research purposes and agendas. The exception is a large body of indigenous knowledges,[2] as well as becomingswith that could be identified as critical animal studies[3] that have been traditionally, and continue to be, placed in the margin. One type of action that we as researchers can take at this point is to becomewith this traditionally marginalized work. These unthought and unpredictable relations would not be as controlling agents or voices for but rather as students who hope to learn from/with both the more than human and traditionally marginalized human knowledges and ways of being.

Equally important is to always and already identify and understand purposeful discourses and actions that attempt (and have been successful at times) to discredit and counter critical scholarly, community, and policy movements toward a more just world. As Collins (2000) reminded us almost 20 years ago, as critical work and resistance become evident related to intersecting oppressions, new forms of power are generated to silence the traditionally oppressed and reinscribe/reinstate power for those who have been predominantly privileged. Combining the work of a range of others (so not for us as original), Lincoln and I discussed in 2009 the backlashes against gains made by the increased openness to multiple knowledges, diverse voices, and ways of being and living evidenced in time periods such as the 1960s civil rights movements. This backlash ranged from redeployment of funds to organized attempts to discredit fields such as ethnic studies, journalism, the judiciary, and education using conservative think tanks to reinscriptions of dominant knowledges through constructs such as evidence-based research and big data (Cannella & Lincoln, 2009).

Yet we have made gains. There have been transformations, not as much for the poor, the more than human, or the environment (which is where we really need to place our activist focus) but rather for researchers and scholars as well as the public discourse in some locations. For those of us who are older, most of our doctoral programs contained no coursework that was critical, and dissertations were at best focused on traditional multicultural perspectives, not diverse forms of thinking, knowing, or being—and certainly not critically related to power, equity, marginalization, or justice. We now have a generation of scholars who have had the opportunity to engage throughout their graduate work with critical perspectives and reconceptualization. Further, some critical discourse, as well as ways of being, are used and accepted by at least some in the public (e.g., the notion that normalization is a problem). There is now an unthought, unpredictable, and oddkin history of actions, critical research, productive critique, languages, and literature that are of value in our becomingswith justice and equity. In addition greater numbers of scholars and activists are now prepared to join these becomingswith movements toward justice.

An Example Critical History of Becomingswith

As an in-depth example of past work, I want to share some of this work from a postcolonial/indigenous project that Kathryn Manuelito (a Diné, Navajo woman indigenous to land only recently labeled the United States) and I (a woman born in the United States but of British descent) published 10 years ago (Cannella & Manuelito, 2008). The project involved our becomingswith the entanglement of Navajo worldviews and qualitative research. After months of getting to know each other, eating together, sharing our lives, and making-with Navajo understandings and the values of critical inquiry, we becamewith each other as beings, immanently reconceptualizing newly related research and education kin. In the following quote, we begin by referring to an anticolonial discussion with Cheryl Rau a few years previous that came to represent our ethical entanglements early on:

> Consistent with the long history of American Indian anticolonialist struggle, Rau (2005), a Máori educator, insisted that the decolonialist perspective actually be referred to as anticolonial social science, a perspective that would challenge the illusion that decolonizing can eliminate the effects of oppression. The notion of anticolonialism then requires an orientation that is radically activist and does not support a false separation between academic research and transformative actions in the contemporary world. (Cannella & Manuelito, 2008, p. 49)

Following this shared value perspective, in our relations and in our text, we go on to propose that our research purposes, teaching, activist practices, thinking, and consciousness be transformed. These reconceptualizations becamewith notions of: (a) ontological transformation, (b) constructing a radically ethical self that would embody a nonviolent revolutionary consciousness (hooks, 2000), (c) egalitarian and collective relations, and (d) direct physical challenges to systems that do not support justice. Obviously, I believe that this anticolonial work is of utmost importance, and I also believe it is directly related to current societal conditions, historically related to contemporary academic activism, and akin to current theoretical perspectives regarding ethics that entangle human/nonhuman worlds (Barad, 2007; Wolfe, 2010). To illustrate, the following provides our expanded thoughts related to one aspect of these reconceptualizations: our multiple becomingswith each other, Navajo worldviews, and the purposes and practices of critical research regarding the nature of reality.

Navajo ontology provides an excellent example of needed researcher transformation in perspective and possibility. Just as critical views broadly have reminded us that conventional postpositivist research tends to represent dominant, White male modernist orientations toward universalist and rational beliefs about reality, entanglements with (and centering of) a traditionally marginalized knowledge require that notions of reality and existence be turned upside down, inside out, or even discarded. Kathryn discusses a Navajo foundation for the nature of being, the ontological orientation:

> I am first and foremost a member of my four clans, which represent my female ancestry, my mother, and grandmother's heritage. I belong to my mother's mother's family for generations previous and time immemorial . . . We are children of Asdzaan Nadleehi (Changing Woman) . . . It is evident when Diné (Navajo) men, women, and children all line up at the end of the Kinaalda, girl's puberty ceremony, to be touched and blessed by the Kinaalda, the girl representing and actually becoming Asdzaan Nadleehi. (Cannella & Manuelito, 2008, p. 51)

For any possibility of becomingswith Navajo and many other indigenous perspectives, one must be open to what the dominant West would tend to label the inconceivable, impossible, and even absurd. For example, the previous quote illustrates that the nature of being for Navajo has been/is ontologically female—with, by the way, a Navajo conceptualization of female. This conceptualization is relational and both animate and inanimate, rather than the hierarchical, dualistic notion of female as constructed by the patriarchal West. Fluid sexual and gender roles are accepted by all, functioning through a woman-oriented egalitarianism (Jaimes Guerrero, 1997). Creation, equality, and life as bodily realm are represented through Changing Woman and do not engage with Western dualisms such as mind/body, male/female, human/nonhuman. In this position, multiple, even contradictory, epistemologies can engage equitably and with caring support

(Cannella & Manuelito, 2008). Further, as an Anglo woman, I know that my becomingswith Kathryn, Navajo perspectives, and research are forever limited by my racial privilege, academic orientation, a childhood embedded in Tennessee mountain views of the world, and so on. Yet however limited I might be, the focus on relations away from my individualism generates unthought and unpredictable ways of being for both present and continued ontological transformations.

Additionally, and very much an issue for researchers, Jaimes (1992) reminded us almost 30 years ago that enlightenment scientific intentions are embedded within the Euro-American error played out in the assumption that one group has the right to represent others. Even qualitative and well-intended research purposes and methods result in errors of misinterpretation and misrepresentation. These include distorted and insulting terminologies such as tribal, primitive, and erotic (Jaimes, 2003). Indigenous knowledges and worldviews could have resulted in all types of becomingswith for many generations. Unfortunately, colonialism has served to disqualify, silence, and even erase these possibilities for centuries—first through physical violence and murder and, more recently, through intellectual denial that diverse ways of being and existing, multiple forms of knowledge, and even different interpretations of thought and understanding have been/are all around us. These denials and erasures also apply to notions of revolutionary ethics and egalitarian relations, as well as challenges to unjust systems. Although contemporary scholars are attempting to place the more than human and justice broadly at the center of our concerns—and, to some extent, rightfully so—Diné relational, egalitarian, and ethical realities, as with many other marginalized groups, have been entangled with these concerns for generations. The concerns are only new to the dominant White, male West. We should absolutely avoid thinking, writing, and acting as if contemporary challenges to human privilege (whether labeled posthuman, more than human, or feminist new materialism) are new or unique. Again, Kathryn further illustrates Navajo ontology as embedded within a connection to the land for time immemorial, although this worldview was/has been at best placed in the margin but most often violently assaulted:

> Land is a macro prototype of our Mother, Changing Woman. Both land and the Hogan are synonymous. Both are "mothers" to our people. Land known as Mother Earth is not a metaphor to Diné.

> Mother Earth is a being who is a source of life, gives birth to all living creatures, and sustains the life of her children by providing them with food and protection. Mother Earth, like our human mothers, is priceless and not a commodity that can be sold or bought as real estate. According to Diné (Navajo) philosophical teachings, land and the environment exist as sacred space. (Cannella & Manuelito, 2008, p. 53)

Further, related to this example of indigenous becomingswith is a 30-year history of environmentalism brought to bear by ecofeminism and its unique epistemologies that assume interconnections between human and nonhuman, life and nonlife, while also directly challenging these embedded dualisms. Examples include India's Chipko (tree-hugging) movement in which the traditional worship of tree goddesses and tree embracing were revived in attempts to save forests from erosion and cash cropping (Shiva, 1988), indigenous actions against intellectual and biopiracy (Mohanty, 1988, 2003; Shiva, 1988), and critiques that have unmasked the ways in which contemporary discourses of sustainable development actually reinforce dominance and do not lead to increased social or environment justice (Braidotti, Charkiewics, Hausler, & Wieringa, 1994). As with most perspectives that challenge the dominant, ecofeminism has been both heavily critiqued (Sargisson, 2001) and most recently robustly defended and supported (Nhanenge, 2011; Sturgeon, 2016). These complexities again leave us with questions regarding perspective, next steps, and actions.

Nurturing Further Critical Relations: Facilitating Posthuman Entanglement

Our next steps can be to open ourselves and our research and actions to becomingswith traditionally marginalized groups of human beings along with becomingswith more-than-human kin, the environment, and collaborative others, to becomingswith critical histories and action—whether academic interventions, locally on the streets, or crossing boundaries nationally and globally. These openings would be to multiplicities that reject right/wrong approaches to criticality and to becomingswith a politics of hope. As I have tried to demonstrate with Haraway's notion of becoming(s)with, past critical work and worldviews should not be in competition with posthuman, more-than-human, or new materialist perspectives, but rather combined for greater previously unthought productivities and possibilities toward increased justice.

From critical work that has demonstrated the privilege for some that is created through enlightenment, modernist patriarchy to notions of hybridity beginning with subaltern survival through the technological cyborg transformation to feminist new materialism to the development of fields such as critical animal studies and critical environmental studies, and so on, these multidirectional philosophical and political perspectives tend to acknowledge intersecting power, privilege, and the experiences of injustice from/in a range of locations. Speaking for myself, I believe that I, as a critical scholar, am morally obligated to both continue and broaden my focus by asking: Is it possible to decenter the human in research, teaching, public policy, and care without creating an environment of postresponsibility for justice for human beings, the environment, and the more-than-human other? To further add to the complexity of our current condition, can there ever be increased equity and justice for human beings if anyone (whether identified as human or nonhuman) continues to be marginalized, used, discredited, mistreated, killed, and/or erased?

There is so much to consider that I totally understand (and often feel myself) the reluctance of many to challenge human privilege in our conceptualizations of research and practices of education and care. Further, critical scholars who are certainly dedicated to the elimination of human social injustices such as poverty, racism, and sexism are rightfully concerned that a postanthropocentric turn may not address the inequities and suffering that continue to exist and are even increasing for many groups of human beings. As Jackson (2015) points out, "the resounding silence in the posthumanist, object-oriented, and new materialist literatures with respect to race is remarkable, persisting even despite the reach of antiblackness into the nonhuman" (p. 216).

To add to these complexities and contradictions, the invasion of neoliberal capitalism into most, if not all, forms of public life is postanthropocentric. All living critters (to use Haraway's word), the environment, and matter have become capital (e.g., whether human capital, resources, the death trophy of violent sports, or knowledges/practices/objects used by the entrepreneur to make money). This all-encompassing notion of capital invades every aspect of life in the name of, not the human, another animal, or the earth, but in the name of competition, profit, and patriarchal power. Neoliberal capitalism is certainly postanthropocentric. Human beings, other forms of life, and even the earth are no longer the center. Rather, capital is the focus. Although discussing neoliberal capitalism is for another volume because of the complexities of power related to its all-invasive practices, understanding that neoliberalism imposes a damaging form of posthumanism on all and everything is an absolute necessity. Further, in addition to recognizing how posthuman neoliberal capitalism impacts our attempts to increase justice, acknowledging posthumanism (and related perspectives) as multidirectional, even diffractive, is important. Posthumanism can focus on increased inclusion, for example, becomingswith the nonhuman beings and objects who have been traditionally excluded. Posthumanism can also be used to reinscribe exclusions, such as further marginalization of people of color and/or increased denials of knowledges that have existed for centuries but have been excluded from both academic recognition and understandings of lived experiences.

So again we face complexities and question ourselves regarding what to do as researchers and educators. I believe that this complex, contradictory, and even dangerous contemporary work that challenges human privilege, whether referred to as posthuman, postanthropocentric, or otherwise, provides concepts, languages, actions, and for some complete reconceptualizations that can be companions with our past critical research and actions to form all manner of becomingswith relations toward justice. In doing so, unthought ways of being and new possibilities can emerge. Increased equity and justice can be achieved as long as we remember, hear, and make-with our critical histories and the voices of diversity that represent the strengths of those histories while we employ posthuman ways of being, literatures, constructs, and possibilities as partners in becomingswith each other. Considering new combinations and relations while always and already attempting to avoid new or reinscribed exclusions can be possible, and these new combinations can even be taken to the public.

As an example, my teaching experiences in the world as well as one of my academic fields are both grounded in a concern for the lives of those who are labeled younger human beings who continue to face marginalization, abuse, inequity, and injustice. I believe that Foucaultian genealogy is a critical event that can intervene in the politics of these conditions. Yet I am also concerned with the power that human beings continue to exert over other living beings and that this power is linked to the treatment of young children. So, I must struggle with ways to becomewith my concerns for both young human beings and our worldly living companions (whether domestic or wild). I begin asking myself questions regarding my intra- and interactions with each and both concerns, as well as the combinations of the concerns, my critical work, and even my understandings of my related strengths and how these becomewith. Ultimately, I may even be trying to address questions such as: What does equity for all children along with placing other living creatures at the center mean for the education of those young children? How is this played out in the learning environments that are created for them or that younger human beings create for themselves? Are other living creatures recognized and supported as agents individually and in becomingwith the children and the environment? What are the intra- and interactions? Further, how might these questions be addressed by combining ideas from indigenous studies, past critical perspectives, and posthuman fields such as critical animal studies? These questions all involve ontological transformation, ethical consciousness, egalitarian relations, and direct actions.

Some scholars are using critical and activist work to decenter the human in their research. One excellent example is the work of Kinard, Gainer, and Huerta (2018), who implement a multicultural, multilingual curriculum for children ages three to eight as a collaboration among Texas State University, the San Marcos schools, the children, the parents of the children, and the material world around everyone. The teacher scholars use past critical work that ranges from Anzaldua to Bhabha, Bloch, Burman, Foucault, Freire, and Espinosa, along with the work of new materialists, posthuman, and assemblage scholars such as Barad, Deleuze, Davies, and Lenz Taguchi (just to name a few) as they becomewith the children in ways that move toward bilingualism as the norm, as well as curriculum as multiple becomings and challenges to our ageist dualisms. This attempt to practice bilingualism as a norm constructs new forms of public research, pedagogy, and activism. Because their project is a public action, the researcher educator activists remind us that after years of attempting to challenge narrow-minded views of diversity, they could no longer stand what they had stood before and decided to "jump willy-nilly into the fray" (Kinard et al., 2018, p. 3).

Another example is the work of Tesar and Arndt (2018) as they address the public policy emphasis on the measurement of quality early childhood programs using a posthuman lens. Recognizing the problem with universalist notions of educational quality that are being imposed globally, the scholars rethink what quality could mean in relation to multiplicities and uncertainties for both human and nonhuman subjects if entangled in ways that challenge the boundaries of human-centric practice. The authors ultimately call for a revolt through which quality would become as a state of change, transformation, entanglement, and continuous probing. Children and the nonhuman world around them would be elevated as powerful agents, listened to, and known for engaging locally and ecologically. Through this conceptualization of quality, a network of professionals, children, nonhuman beings, and diverse critical ideas could becomewith a new notion and practice of quality.

We could find many other examples where researchers, educators, and community workers attempt to combine diverse critical perspectives and ways of being to challenge and cross the boundaries of human centeredness, various forms of oppression, politics, and even capitalism. The work has just begun. Finally, although critical perspectives have for decades acknowledged that everything is political, our focus contemporarily must also be about how to literally becomewith a politics of hope. Perhaps entangling posthuman concerns with our past critical work can create new avenues and new openings for keeping our activist hope alive. By keeping the strength and connections that form critical community, whatever community means for each of us (e.g., local, global, collective, part of the knowledge community with which we work, within our relations and entanglements), increased justice, social or otherwise, is always/already possible.

1 Contemporary critical scholarship has begun to place an emphasis on justice and equity in relation to living creatures that have not been identified as human. These bodies of literature are identified as posthuman, more than human, postanthropocentric, and even beyond human. Also included are perspectives that are concerned with the environment and the valuing of the earth, as well as what is now labeled feminist new materialism. These perspectives are not identical but do share the concern that so-called human beings have continuously been privileged over other creatures, objects, and the earth, as well as agental relations and intra- and interactions. See scholars listed in this chapter such as Barad, Braidotti, Haraway, and Wolff, as well as indigenous knowledges and scholars. Although there are diverse views of posthumanism, in this text I use the range of labels that would attempt to decenter the human.

2 See the following indigenous scholars: Gandhi, Jaimes, Mohanty, Said, Smith, and Spivak.
3 See the following for a discussion of critical animal studies by McCance (2013) and Nocella, Sorenson, Socha, and Matsuoka (2013) as well as methods such as multispecies ethnography and critiques of speciesism.</ftn>

References

Anzaldúa, G. (1987). *Borderlands/La frontera.* San Francisco, CA: Spinsters/Aunt Lute.
Anzaldúa, G. (Ed.) (1990). *Making face, making soul.* San Francisco, CA: Aunt Lute.
Barad, K. (2007). *Meeting the universe halfway: Quantum physics and the entanglement of matter and meaning.* Durham, NC: Duke University Press.
Bayoumi, M. (2018). The drowning years: To be Muslim and American in the age of Trump is to live in a state of constant dread. *The Nation, 306*(3), 12-15.
Black Lives Matter. (n.d.). *About the Black Lives Matter network.* Retrieved from https://blacklivesmatter.com
Braidotti, R., Charkiewicz, E., Hausler, S., & Wieringa, S. (1994). *Women, the environment, and sustainable development.* London, UK: Zed Books.
Butler, J. (1993). *Bodies that matter: On the discursive limits of "sex."* New York, NY: Routledge.
Cannella, G. S. (2015). Engaging critical qualitative science: Histories and possibilities. In G. S. Cannella, M. Salazar Perez, & P. A. Pasque (Eds.), *Critical qualitative inquiry: Foundations and futures* (pp. 7-28). Walnut Creek, CA: Left Coast Press.
Cannella, G. S., & Lincoln, Y. (2009). Deploying qualitative methods for critical social purposes. In N. K. Denzin & M. D. Giardina (Eds.), *Qualitative inquiry and social justice* (pp. 53-72). Walnut Creek, CA: Left Coast Press.
Cannella, G. S., & Manuelito, K. (2008). Feminisms from unthought locations: Indigenous worldviews, marginalized feminisms, and revisioning an anticolonial social science. In N. K. Denzin, Y. S. Lincoln, & L. T. Smith (Eds.), *Handbook of critical and indigenous methodologies* (pp. 45-59). Thousand Oaks, CA: Sage.
Collins, P. H. (2000). *Black feminist thought: Knowledge, consciousness, and the politics of empowerment.* New York, NY: Routledge.
Costain, A. N. (1992). *Inviting women's rebellion.* Baltimore, MD: Johns Hopkins University Press.
Folkers, A. (2016). Daring the truth: Foucault, parrhesia, and the genealogy of critique. *Theory, Culture, and Society, 33*(1), 3-28.
Foucault, M. (1997). What is critique? In S. Lotringer & L. Hochroth (Eds.), *The politics of truth* (pp. 41-81). New York, NY: Semiotext(e).

Foucault, M. (2003). *Society must be defended: Lectures at the College de France, 1975-1976* (D. Macoy, Trans.). New York, NY: Picador.
Gandhi, L. (1998). *Postcolonial theory: A critical introduction.* New York, NY: Columbia University Press.
Gandhi, M. K. (2001). *Non-violent resistance* (Satyagraha). Mineola, NY: Dover Publications. Original publication 1951.
Hannam, J. (2005). International dimensions of women's suffrage: At the crossroads of several interlocking identities. *Women's History Review, 14*(3-4), 543-560.
Haraway, D. J. (2008). *When species meet.* Minneapolis, MN: University of Minnesota Press.
Haraway, D. J. (2016). *Staying with the trouble: Making kin in the Chthulucene.* Durham, NC: Duke University Press.
Harding, S. (1986). *The science question in feminism.* Ithaca, NY: Cornell University Press.
hooks, b. (2000). *Feminism is for everybody: Passionate politics.* Cambridge, MA: South End Press.
Jackson, Z. I. (2015). Outer worlds: The persistence of race in movement "beyond the human." *GLQ: A Journal of Lesbian and Gay Studies, 21*(2-3), 215-218.
Jaimes, M. A. (1992). La raza and indigenism: Alternatives to autogenocide in North America. *Global Justice, 3*(2-3), 4-19.
Jaimes, M. A. (2003). "Patriarchal colonialism" and "indigenism": Implications for native feminist spirituality and native womanism. *Hypatia—A Journal of Feminist Philosophy, 18*(2). Retrieved from http://rdsweb1.rdsinc.com.ezproxy1.libasu.edu/texis/rds/suite2/+sceJjD63mxwwwwwFqz6
Jaimes Guerrero, M. A. (1997). Civil rights versus sovereignty: Native American women in life and land struggles. In M. J. Alexander & C. T. Mohanty (Eds.), *Feminist genealogies, colonial legacies, democratic futures* (pp. 101-121). New York, NY: Routledge.
Kinard, T., Gainer, J., & Huerta, M. E. S. (2018). *Power play: Explorando y empujando fronteras en una escuela en Tejas through a multilingual play-based early learning curriculum.* New York, NY: Peter Lang.
King, M. L. (1959, July). My trip to the land of Gandhi. *Ebony,* pp. 84-92. The Martin Luther King Papers Project. Retrieved from kingencyclopedia.stanford.edu/primarydocuments/Vol5/July1959_MyTriptotheLandofGandhi.pdf
Latour, B. (2004). Why has critique run out of steam? From matters of fact to matters of concern. *Critical Inquiry, 30*(2), 225-248.
Lopez, G. (2017). A new FBI report says hate crimes—especially against Muslims—went up in 2016. *Vox.* Retrieved from https://www.vox.com/identities/2017/11/13/16643448/fbi-hate-crimes-2016
McCance, D. (2013). *Critical animal studies: Introduction.* New York, NY: State University of New York Press.

Mohanty, C. T. (1988). Under Western eyes: Feminist scholarship and colonial discourses. *Feminist Review, 30*, 60-88.

Mohanty, C. T. (2003). *Feminism without borders: Decolonizing theory, practicing solidarity.* Durham, NC: Duke University Press.

Morris, A. D. (1984). *The origins of the civil rights movement: Black communities organizing for change.* New York, NY: The Free Press.

National Geographic. (2018). A running list of how Trump is changing the environment. Retrieved from https://news.nationalgeographic.com/2017/03/how-trump-is-changing-science-environment.html

Nhanenge, J. (2011). *Ecofeminism: Towards integrating the concerns of women, poor people, and native into development.* Lanham, MD: University Press of America.

Nocella, A. J., Sorenson, J., Socha, K., & Matsuoka, A. (Eds.). (2014). *Defining critical animal studies: An intersectional social justice approach for liberation.* New York, NY: Peter Lang.

Noys, B. (2011, November). The discreet charm of Bruno Latour, or the critique of "anti-critique." Presented at the Centre for Critical Theory, University of Nottingham. Retrieved from www.academia.edu/1477950/The_Discret_Charm_of_Bruno_Latour_or_the_critique_of_anti-critique

Pankhurst, E. (1913, November 13). Freedom or death. Speech delivered on the streets of Hartford, CT. Reproduced in *The Guardian*, April 27, 2007. Retrieved from https://www.theguardian.com/theguardian/2007/apr/27/greatspeeches

Piven, F. F., & Cloward, R. A. (1977). *Poor people's movements: Why they succeed, how they fail.* New York, NY: Vintage Books.

Rau, C. (2005, October). *Indigenous metaphors of the heart: Transformative praxis in early childhood education in Aotearoa, privileging Māori women's educator's voices.* Paper presented at the 13th International Conference on Reconceptualizing Early Childhood Research Theory and Practice, Madison, WI.

Ray, A., & Selinger, E. (2008). Jagannath's Saligram: On Bruno Latour and literary critique after postcoloniality. *Postmodern Culture, 18*(2). Retrieved from http://pmc.iath.virginia.edu/text-only/issue.108/18.2ray_selinger.txt

Said, E. (1978). *Orientalism.* London, UK: Routledge and Kegan Paul.

Sargisson, L. (2001). What's wrong with ecofeminism? *Environmental Studies, 10*(1), 52-64.

Shiva, V. (1988). *Staying alive: Women, ecology, and development.* London, UK: Zed Books.

Smith, L. T. (1999/2012). *Decolonizing methodologies: Research and indigenous peoples.* London, UK: Zed Books.

Snow, D. A., Soule, S. A., & Kriesi, H. (Eds.). (2004). *The Blackwell companion to social movements.* Oxford, UK: Blackwell.

Spivak, G. C. (1988). Can the subaltern speak? In C. Nelson & L. Grossberg (Eds.), *Marxism and the interpretation of culture* (pp. 271-313). Urbana, IL: University of Illinois Press.

Sturgeon, N. (2016). *Ecofeminist natures: Race, gender, feminist theory, and political action*. New York, NY: Routledge.

Tesar, M., & Arndt, S. (2018). Posthuman childhoods: Questions concerning quality. In M. Bloch, B. B. Swadener, & G. S. Cannella (Eds.), *Reconceptualizing early childhood care and education: Critical questions, diverse imaginaries, and social activism* (pp. 113-128). New York, NY: Peter Lang.

von Werlhof, C. (2007). Capitalist patriarchy and the negation of matriarchy: The struggle for a "deep" alternative. In G. Vaughan (Ed.), *Women and the gift economy: A radically different world view is possible* (pp. 139-153). Toronto, Canada: Inanna.

Wolfe, C. (2010). *What is posthumanism?* Minneapolis, MN: University of Minnesota Press.

Wolfe, C. (2013). *Before the law: Humans and other animals in a biopolitical frame*. Chicago, IL: The University of Chicago Press.

Afterword

Pedagogies of Hope for Dark Days: Talking Points

Norman K. Denzin

IT REMAINS TO return to the beginning, to take up again the task of offering a critical framework for reading performance ethnography's place in a progressive discourse that advances a pedagogy of freedom and hope in this 21st century. We seek to understand the world, but we demand a performative politics that leads the way to radical social change. We have fallen prey to a politics of extremism, misogyny, and ultranationalism (Giroux, 2016).

1. We need a dignified politics that is "open to the possibilit[ies] of nonviolent ways of living" (Giroux, 2016, p. 219).

2. We need a community-centered democracy that promotes civic literacy and encourages alignments between protest movements led by youth, women, Latinos, Muslims, LGBT persons, the poor, perhaps modeled after the Black Lives Matter movement. Now, more than ever, we need reasons to believe that citizens can reclaim their voice in the public sphere, where they can speak out, protest, express their outrage, and voice their utopian dreams of peace and justice.

3. We must use our analytical skills to imagine "more equitable and just societies," while shaping democratic ideals and inspiring civic courage (Giroux, 2016, p. 222).

4. We need a public pedagogy that emphasizes an ethics of trust, compassion, care, and solidarity.

5. We need to fight off despair, self-pity, and fear. We must model creative resistance.

6. We must work to imagine better futures and new ways of sustainable living in "one world in which many worlds fit" as the Zapatista of Mexico envision it (Giroux, 2016, p. 223).

7. We must forge a "banner of solidarity for real ideological and structural change" (Giroux, 2016, p. 57). This would be a discourse willing to "unite [the] fragmented Left around the call for a resurgent insurrectional democracy" (p. 58). "Embraces cannot support a democratic society" at all (p. 58).

8. We must encourage the development of critical historical memories.

9. We must mobilize against the violence of organized forgetting. We must stop the willful erasure and distortion of radical discourses that encourage critical thinking (Giroux, 2000). We must mobilize students to be critically engaged historical agents, attentive to important social issues.

10. Critical pedagogy teaches students how to critique a social order, like the Tucson school district that banned Paulo Freire's (2000) *Pedagogy of the Oppressed* and dismantled its Mexican American Studies Program (Giroux, 2016).

11. Students must be taught that inquiry is always about power, about what is knowledge, about what is truth—that is, inquiry is always a form of moral intervention in the service of liberation.

12. We cannot separate theories, values, and inquiry from moral and ethical and political being (Giroux, 2016). The challenge is to inspire people to

become critical inquirers and critically engaged citizens willing to fight for democracy, liberation, and solidarity (Giroux, 2016).

13. We seek students and researchers who embrace a politics of emancipation.

14. We seek leaders who will help us enact a pedagogy of educated hope.

15. We need teachers who as public intellectuals will teach students how to be critical historical agents.

16. We need students who are not afraid to raise their voices in solidarity with those who struggle to translate personal troubles into public issues (Giroux, 2016; Mills, 1959).

17. We must defend the public sphere. We need history lessons, remembering moments in the past when resistance was required—the labor strikes of 1930s, the civil rights movement of the 1950s and 1960s, the antiwar new left movement of the 1960s, the women's liberation movement of the 1960s and 1970s, the LGBT rights movement of the 1960s and 1970s, the contemporary Black Lives Matter movement.

18. We need to reclaim a radical democratic imagination that sees democracy as a never-ending struggle. We need an ongoing language of critique, of hope, a broad-based democratic liberation movement with many rhizomatic roots, trunks, and branches (Giroux, 2016).

19. We need a *new geography of hope* to help our suffering souls in these times of spiritual crisis, hate crimes, swastikas, and racial intolerance (Stegner, 1980).

***

These are the troubled spaces that radical performance autoethnography must enter.

References

Freire, P. (2000). *Pedagogy of the oppressed,* 30th anniversary edition, with an Introduction by Donaldo Macedo. New York, NY: Continuum. Originally published 1970.

Giroux, H. (2000). *Impure acts: The practical politics of cultural studies.* New York, NY: Routledge.

Giroux, H. (2016). *America at war with itself.* San Francisco, CA: City Lights Open Media.

Mills, C. W. (1959). *The sociological imagination.* New York, NY: Oxford.

Stegner, W. (1980). Coda: Wilderness letter. *The sound of mountain water: The changing American West* (pp. 145–153). New York, NY: Doubleday.

List of Contributors

Gaile S. Cannella (EdD, University of Georgia) is an independent scholar who has served as a tenured full professor at Texas A&M University–College Station and at Arizona State University–Tempe, as well as the Velma Schmidt Endowed Chair of Education at the University of North Texas. Her doctoral students have received outstanding dissertation awards from the American Educational Research Association. Dr. Cannella's scholarship focuses on diverse constructions of critical qualitative inquiry, reconceptualist childhood studies and education, and justice broadly, including related to environmental studies and the more-than-human. Dr. Cannella's work has appeared in a range of journals and volumes, including *Qualitative Inquiry, Cultural Studies <=> Critical Methodologies,* and *International Review of Qualitative Research*. Her most recent books are *Critical Qualitative Research Reader* (Peter Lang, 2012) with Shirley Steinberg; *Reconceptualizing Early Childhood Care and Education* (Peter Lang, 2014, 2nd edition 2018) with Marianne Bloch and Beth Swadener; *Critical Qualitative Inquiry: Foundations and Futures* (Left Coast Press, 2015) with Michelle Pérez and Penny Pasque; and *Critical Examinations of Quality in Childhood Education and Care* (Peter Lang, 2016) with Michelle Pérez and I-Fang Lee. She is currently working on research projects that include early years critical perspectives in education, and critical qualitative inquiry as public activisms and unthought imaginary. Dr. Cannella received the 2017 Reconceptualizing Early Childhood Education and Care Bloch Career Award.

Bronwyn Davies is an independent scholar, a professorial fellow at the University of Melbourne and an Emeritus Professor at Western Sydney University. She is a writer, scholar, and teacher and has been a visiting professor in the last few years in the United States, Sweden, Denmark, Belgium, Finland, and the UK. She is well known for her work using collective biography; her work on gender, literacy, and pedagogy; and her critique of neoliberalism as it impacts on university work. Her most recent book is *Listening to Children: Being and Becoming* (Routledge, 2014). She is currently writing a three-volume book based on the lives of her ancestors. More details of her work can be found on her website, bronwyndavies.com.au

Norman K. Denzin is Professor Emeritus of Communications, College of Communications, and Research Professor of Communications, Sociology, and Humanities at the University of Illinois, Urbana-Champaign. One of the world's foremost authorities on qualitative research and cultural criticism, Denzin is the author or editor of more than two dozen books, including *The Qualitative Manifesto: A Call to Arms* (Routledge, 2010), *Qualitative Inquiry Under Fire: Toward a New Paradigm Dialogue* (Routledge, 2017), *Searching for Yellowstone: Race, Gender, Family, and Memory in the Postmodern West* (Routledge, 2016), *Reading Race: Hollywood and the Cinema of Racial Violence* (Sage, 2015); *Interpretive Ethnography: Ethnographic Practices for the 21st Century* (Sage, 2015), *The Cinematic Society: The Voyeur's Gaze* (Sage, 1995), and *The Alcoholic Society: Addiction and Recovery of the Self* (Routledge, 2017). He is past editor of *The Sociological Quarterly*, co-editor (with Yvonna S. Lincoln) of four editions of the landmark *Handbook of Qualitative Research*, co-editor (with Michael D. Giardina) of five plenary volumes from the annual *Congress of Qualitative Inquiry*, co-editor (with Lincoln) of the methods journal *Qualitative Inquiry*, founding editor of *Cultural Studies <=> Critical Methodologies* and *International Review of Qualitative Research*, and editor of three book series.

Madison Hayes is the executive director of the Refugee Community Partnership in Carrboro, North Carolina. She teaches paradigms of social change to undergraduate students at the University of North Carolina–Chapel Hill and is a community organizer with Organizing Against Racism NC. Madison is a 2018 Fellow with the Los Angeles–based Roddenberry Foundation, which supports a national ecosystem of change makers, disruptors, and activists.

M. Francyne Huckaby (PhD, Texas A&M University) is professor of curriculum studies; core faculty of Women and Gender Studies, Africana and African American Studies, and Comparative Race and Ethnic Studies; and previous Center for Public Education director at Texas Christian University. Her forthcoming book is *Researching Resistance: Public Education After Neoliberalism* (Myers Education Press, forthcoming), and other work appears in various journals and edited books. She received TCU's Women and Gender Studies Claudia V. Camp Faculty Research and Creative Activity Award and the American Educational Research Association Outstanding Dissertation of the Year Award (Qualitative Research SIG) for

Challenging the Hegemony in Education: Specific Parrhesiastic Scholars, Care of the Self, and Relations of Power (2005).

Mirka Koro-Ljungberg (PhD, University of Helsinki) is a professor of qualitative research at Arizona State University. Her scholarship operates in the intersection of methodology, philosophy, and socio-cultural critique, and her work aims to contribute to methodological knowledge, experimentation, and theoretical development across various traditions associated with qualitative research. She has published in various qualitative and educational journals, and she is the author of *Reconceptualizing Qualitative Research: Methodologies Without Methodology* (Sage, 2016) and co-editor of *Disrupting Data in Qualitative Inquiry: Entanglements With the Post-Critical and Post-Anthropocentric* (Peter Lang, 2017).

Luz Zareth Moreno is a PhD student at the Research Center for Applied Communication (CICA), Anahuac University, Mexico City. Her doctoral thesis focuses on the children literacies appropriations in marginalized populations. Her current research is centered on social representations, cultural studies, and contemporary social theories from the qualitative point of view. She is co-author of the book *El Modelo Comunicativo* (Editorial Trillas, 2006).

Joy Pierce is associate professor in the Department of Writing and Rhetoric Studies at the University of Utah. Her digital divides and digital literacies research employs critical cultural and contemporary social theories as well as qualitative research methods to interrogate inequities in digital media use among historically marginalized populations. Her works have been presented at national and international conferences. She has published in communication, sociology, and qualitative methods journals and authored *Digital Fusion: A Society Beyond Blind Inclusion* (Peter Lang, 2015). Her next book, *Autoethnography: Beyond the Self* (Routledge, forthcoming), is expected to be released by early 2019.

Hillary Rubesin is the executive director of the Art Therapy Institute in Carrboro, North Carolina. She is a registered expressive arts therapist and a licensed professional counselor (LCP), currently working toward her doctorate at Lesley University. Since 2008, Hillary has worked primarily with refugees and immigrants from various countries resettling in North Carolina.

Jasmine Brooke Ulmer (PhD, University of Florida) is an assistant professor of education evaluation and research at Wayne State University in Detroit. Her research interests include writing, pedagogy, and critical qualitative inquiry. Prior to entering postsecondary education, she served as an instructional coach, national board-certified teacher, and classroom policy fellow at the U.S. Department of Education.

Franklin Vernon is a graduate program coordinator and faculty member in the Department of Geography, Planning, and Recreation at Northern Arizona University. He holds a PhD from Indiana University School of Public Health and was previously a postdoctoral fellow with University of Wisconsin School of Education and Wisconsin HOPE Lab, and faculty with Northwestern University Feinberg School of Medicine. He strives to be a transdisciplinary scholar, drawing from across the social sciences and humanities to inform his work in critical ethnography and educational justice.